AI - The Tsunami of Opportunities - Don't Watch, Ride the Wave!

ZIAD M. ALSUKAIRY

ZIAD M. ALSUKAIRY

CONTENTS

ACKNOWLEDGMENTS

Writing this book has been an incredible journey—one that wouldn't have been possible without the unwavering support, patience, and contributions of those who stood by me every step of the way.

First and foremost, I want to express my deepest gratitude to my family, especially Irina, Tarryk, and Mhamad, whose encouragement, understanding, and belief in this project gave me the strength to push forward. Tarryk and Mhamad, your keen eye for detail and expertise in technology and English literature played a crucial role in shaping this book into what it is today. Your meticulous proofreading, editing, and insightful feedback elevated the content, ensuring that every concept was both clear and compelling.

To everyone who contributed—whether through discussions, feedback, or simply offering words of encouragement—I thank you. Writing about AI in a way that is engaging, accessible, and meaningful is no small task, and this book is the result of collaboration, dedication, and countless hours of hard work.

Finally, to you, the reader—thank you for embarking on this journey into the world of AI. May this book equip you with the knowledge and confidence to ride the wave of opportunities that AI brings.

INTRODUCTION

Why This Book & Why Now?

The Wake-Up Call: AI Is Here, and It Won't Wait for You

Imagine standing on a beach, feeling the pull of the ocean as a **massive wave** approaches. You have two choices—**ride it** or get **dragged under**.

That wave is **artificial intelligence (AI)**. And make no mistake—it's already crashing onto the shore.

In just a few short years, AI has gone from a **buzzword** to a **game-changer**, reshaping industries, workplaces, education, and even the way families function. It's in **your phone, your search results, your social media feed, your workplace tools**, and soon, it will be in nearly every aspect of life.

The scary part? **Most people aren't ready.**

Some are **watching from the sidelines**, uncertain whether to embrace AI or fear it. Others **dismiss it as a passing trend**, thinking it won't affect them. And then there are those who are **riding the wave**—using AI to work smarter, learn faster, and stay ahead.

Which one are you?

This book exists for one reason: **to make sure you're not left behind.**

The Biggest Mistake You Can Make—Ignoring AI

Let's be blunt—**AI is not a fad, and it's not going away.** It's as significant as the **internet, the smartphone, and electricity.**

In business? AI is already automating workflows, analyzing market trends, and personalizing customer experiences.

In education? AI-powered tutors are helping students learn math, science, and languages with **instant feedback and adaptive learning paths.**

At home? AI can manage your schedules, assist with parenting decisions, and even help your kids prepare for the **SATs or learn to code.**

The people who **learn how to use AI** will have an **unfair advantage.** Those who ignore it? **They risk becoming obsolete.**

Now, before you start panicking, let's clear up a common misconception—**AI is not here to replace you.**

It's here to **amplify your potential.**

The people who will thrive in the AI era aren't the ones who **compete with AI**, but the ones who **learn how to work with it.**

This book will show you how.

Why This Book? What You'll Gain

You don't need a **computer science degree** or years of tech experience to understand AI. You just need **the right guide**—and that's exactly what this book is.

Here's what you'll get:

- **A simple, no-nonsense explanation of AI**—no technical jargon, just clear insights.
- **A hands-on guide to the most powerful AI tools today**—including ChatGPT, DeepSeek, Gemini, and Grok.
- **A roadmap for using AI in your daily life**—whether you're a **student, a parent, a professional, or an entrepreneur.**
- **A step-by-step breakdown of AI's role in education, business, career growth, and decision-making.**
- **The skills you need to "talk to AI" effectively**—so you get **real value** instead of useless, generic responses.

This isn't just about understanding AI. **It's about using it to your advantage.**

Who This Book Is For

- ★ You, if you're a beginner who feels lost but wants to learn AI in a practical way.
- ★ You, if you're a parent who wants to prepare your kids for an AI-driven world.
- ★ You, if you're a professional looking to stay competitive in a rapidly changing job market.
- ★ You, if you're an entrepreneur or business owner who wants to harness AI for growth.

This book was written for **real people**—not just tech enthusiasts, but **anyone who wants to be smarter, faster, and more efficient with AI.**

If that's you, then you're in the right place.

Final Call to Action: Ride the Wave!

The future isn't **coming—it's already here.** The question is, **are you ready?**

You have two choices:

1. Ignore AI, hope it doesn't affect you, and risk falling behind.
2. Embrace AI, learn how to use it, and position yourself for success.

This book will help you do the latter.

So don't just **watch from the shore. Jump in, ride the wave, and let's explore how AI can shape your future**—starting now.

CHAPTER 1: AI—THE REVOLUTION THAT'S CHANGING EVERYTHING

The AI Revolution Has Begun—And It's Bigger Than You Think

Imagine waking up one morning to find that **half the world has already changed**—but nobody sent you a memo. That's exactly what's happening with **artificial intelligence (AI)**.

For years, AI was something we associated with **sci-fi movies, tech labs, and futuristic predictions**. But suddenly, it's everywhere—**writing emails, diagnosing diseases, designing marketing campaigns, even helping kids with their homework.**

The AI revolution isn't coming. **It's already here.** And it's moving **faster than the internet boom of the early 2000s** or the **smartphone explosion of the 2010s.**

Think about it:

- **It took the telephone 75 years** to reach 100 million users.
- **It took Facebook 4.5 years** to do the same.
- **ChatGPT? Just 2 months.**

That's how fast AI is transforming the world. **And the biggest mistake you can make? Ignoring it.**

But let's clear something up: AI isn't just about **robots and self-driving cars.** It's about **how we work, how we learn, how we make decisions, and even how we create.**

In this chapter, we'll break down **what AI really is, how it's already shaping industries**, and **why it's something you can't afford to overlook.**

What Is AI, Really? (No Jargon, Just Clarity)

Let's be real—when most people hear the term **"artificial intelligence,"** they imagine some kind of supercomputer plotting to take over the world. But that's Hollywood.

So, what is AI **really?**

At its core, **AI is a system that mimics human intelligence to solve problems, recognize patterns, and make decisions.**

Think of it this way:

- ➤ **Traditional software** is like a **calculator**—it follows **pre-programmed rules** to give you an answer.
- ➤ **AI, on the other hand, learns from experience**—it adapts, predicts, and even generates new ideas.

Breaking It Down Further: AI vs. Traditional Software

Feature	Traditional Software	Artificial Intelligence
How it works	Follows fixed rules	Learns from patterns & data

Example	A calculator solving 2+2	ChatGPT writing an entire essay
Flexibility	Limited—does what it's told	Can generate, predict, and improve responses over time

So, when you chat with **ChatGPT, DeepSeek, Gemini, or Grok**, you're not **just talking to a machine**. You're interacting with an AI that has been trained on **billions of words, facts, and human conversations.**

And that's what makes AI **so powerful**—it's not just following commands, it's **thinking, learning, and generating new ideas** in a way that software never could before.

How AI Is Already Changing Your Life (Even If You Don't Realize It)

You don't need to be a programmer to be using AI. In fact, **you already are**—you just might not realize it.

AI in Healthcare

- AI is detecting diseases **earlier than human doctors**—helping diagnose cancer and predicting heart attacks.
- AI chatbots like **Watson Health** assist doctors by analyzing **millions of medical records in seconds**.

AI in Business & Finance

- AI helps banks **detect fraud** by recognizing unusual spending patterns.
- AI-driven assistants **automate emails, meetings, and even customer service**.

- Investors are using AI to **predict stock market trends** faster than ever before.

AI in Education

- Students use **ChatGPT** to **explain tough concepts in plain English**.
- AI-powered tutors **generate personalized study plans** based on learning strengths and weaknesses.
- Platforms like **Khan Academy AI** offer **real-time feedback on assignments**.

AI in Creativity & Entertainment

- AI is **writing music, generating art, and even directing short films**.
- AI-powered platforms like **Midjourney & DALL·E** create **stunning digital artwork in seconds**.
- AI tools like **Runway ML** allow anyone to create **professional-level video edits with zero experience**.

AI in Everyday Life

- Google Maps uses AI to **predict traffic jams** before they happen.
- AI assistants like **Alexa and Siri** control smart homes, answer questions, and even tell jokes.
- AI-powered chatbots are handling **customer service, scheduling, and task management**.

So, even if you think **AI doesn't affect you**, it already does.

And it's **only going to get bigger**.

AI Myths That Need to Be Debunked Right Now

There's a lot of fear around AI—some of it valid, but much of it based on **misconceptions**. Let's clear up a few things:

Myth #1: "AI is going to take all our jobs!"

➔ AI won't replace **all** jobs—it will replace **tasks**. The people who know **how to use AI** will become **more valuable**, not obsolete.

Myth #2: "AI is only for tech people!"

➔ AI is becoming **as easy to use as a smartphone**—if you can type a question into Google, you can use AI.

Myth #3: "AI is just hype and will fade away."

➔ AI is evolving **faster than the Internet did**—and it's already embedded in every major industry.

Still skeptical? Look at **self-driving cars**, **AI-powered customer service**, and **AI-assisted healthcare**.

This isn't **some future possibility**—it's happening **right now**.

Why You Can't Ignore AI Anymore

If history has taught us anything, it's that **technology waits for no one**.

Those who ignored the internet? **They struggled to adapt.**
Those who dismissed smartphones? **They got left behind.**
And those who assume AI won't impact them? **They're in for a wake-up call.**

AI will **reshape every industry**, and those who **learn it now** will **stay ahead**.

The most **dangerous mindset** you can have is **thinking AI won't affect you**.

It will. **It already is.**

The question is: **Will you take advantage of it, or will you let it pass you by?**

What's Next? (A Sneak Peek at the Rest of This Book)

In the next chapters, we'll dive deeper into:

1. **The top AI chatbots you need to know**—ChatGPT, DeepSeek, Gemini, and Grok.
2. **How AI is helping students, parents, and professionals** improve their skills.
3. **How AI can make your family smarter**—from school to finance to decision-making.

This is your **chance to ride the wave** of AI.

Are you ready?

Turn the page, and let's get started.

CHAPTER 2: MEET THE AI ASSISTANTS – CHATBOTS THAT THINK LIKE HUMANS

The Rise of AI Chatbots: More Than Just Fancy Tech

Imagine having a **personal assistant available 24/7**—one that can help you write emails, summarize books, solve math problems, brainstorm ideas, and even chat with you about history, business, or philosophy. Sounds futuristic, right?

Well, **that future is already here.**

AI chatbots like **ChatGPT, DeepSeek, Gemini, and Grok** are rapidly changing the way people interact with technology. Unlike traditional search engines, these AI assistants **don't just give you links—they understand** your questions, **generate human-like responses**, and even **adapt to your style and preferences** over time.

But here's the big question: **Which AI chatbot is best for you?**

In this chapter, we'll break down **what these AI chatbots can do, how they differ, and how you can use them to your advantage.**

What Are AI Chatbots and How Do They Work?

Before we dive into the top AI assistants, let's get one thing clear—**AI chatbots are NOT just advanced versions of Google Search.**

They are **Large Language Models (LLMs)** trained on **massive amounts of text** from books, articles, research papers, and online discussions.

Here's how they work in simple terms:

1. **Understanding Your Input** – When you type a question, the chatbot **analyzes your words, context, and intent.**
2. **Predicting the Best Response** – Instead of "looking up" an answer, the AI **generates a response based on patterns it has learned** from billions of words.
3. **Refining & Adapting** – Some chatbots, like ChatGPT and Gemini, can **remember parts of your conversation** and adjust their responses accordingly.

So, while Google Search gives you **links to explore**, AI chatbots give you **direct, human-like answers**—often in **seconds**.

ChatGPT – The Conversational Powerhouse

What Is ChatGPT?

ChatGPT, developed by **OpenAI**, is the world's most popular AI chatbot. First released in **November 2022**, it quickly became a **global phenomenon**, gaining **100 million users** in just two months.

At its core, ChatGPT is designed to be **conversational, flexible, and highly creative**. It can:

- Answer questions on **any topic** (science, history, business, etc.)
- Write **essays, emails, resumes, and reports**
- Generate **stories, poems, jokes, and creative content**
- Explain **complex topics in simple terms**

- Assist with **coding, math, and problem-solving**

Strengths of ChatGPT

1. **User-friendly and intuitive** – Anyone can use it without technical knowledge.
2. **Great for writing and brainstorming** – It can generate creative and structured content.
3. **Highly conversational** – Feels more human-like than most AI models.

Limitations of ChatGPT

1. **Not always accurate** – It can generate incorrect or outdated information.
2. **Doesn't browse the web in free version** – Some facts might be missing.
3. **May generate biased responses** – Since it's trained on human content, biases can sometimes show up.

Best Uses for ChatGPT

1. Writing **essays, articles, and social media content**
2. Generating **creative ideas** for projects, scripts, or books
3. Learning **complex topics in a simplified way**
4. Practicing **languages, coding, and problem-solving**

DeepSeek – The Fact-Checking AI for Research & Accuracy

What Is DeepSeek?

DeepSeek is an AI chatbot designed to **prioritize accuracy, research-based answers, and factual precision**. Unlike ChatGPT, which sometimes makes **guesses**, DeepSeek is built to focus on **providing reliable, data-driven responses**.

It's widely used by:

1. **Students and researchers** looking for **accurate summaries** of scientific studies.
2. **Business analysts** who need fact-based insights.
3. **People who value accuracy over creativity.**

Strengths of DeepSeek

1. **Highly accurate and research-driven** – Focuses on providing factual answers.
2. **Great for academic and technical queries** – Ideal for students, scientists, and professionals.
3. **More resistant to misinformation** – Less likely to generate false information.

Limitations of DeepSeek

1. **Less conversational than ChatGPT** – Feels more robotic and factual.
2. **Not as creative** – Not ideal for brainstorming or storytelling.
3. **Still not perfect** – Can still make errors, so fact-checking is necessary.

Best Uses for DeepSeek

1. Researching **academic papers, historical facts, or technical information**
2. Generating **structured, well-referenced reports**
3. Avoiding **misinformation in professional work**

Gemini – Google's AI Assistant for Multimodal Learning

What Is Gemini?

Gemini (formerly Bard) is **Google's advanced AI assistant**. Unlike ChatGPT and DeepSeek, Gemini is **multimodal**—which means it can process and understand **text, images, audio, and even code.**

Strengths of Gemini

1. **Handles text, images, and voice commands** – More than just a chatbot.
2. **Integrates with Google tools** – Works well with Gmail, Docs, and YouTube.
3. **Great for structured content generation** – Helps professionals organize information.

Limitations of Gemini

1. Not as naturally conversational as ChatGPT.
2. Some responses may be filtered or restricted.
3. Web-based, not as widely used as ChatGPT.

Best Uses for Gemini

1. Creating **visual + text-based presentations**
2. Helping with **research and summarizing online data**
3. Integrating AI with **Google services**

Grok – Elon Musk's AI With Attitude

What Is Grok?

Grok, developed by **xAI (Elon Musk's company)**, is designed to be **more opinionated, humorous, and integrated with Twitter/X.**

Strengths of Grok

1. Connected to real-time Twitter/X data – Great for news updates.
2. More conversational and witty – Less robotic, more engaging.
3. Designed for quick, short-form content.

Limitations of Grok

1. Not ideal for research or technical work.
2. More opinionated, less neutral.
3. Still developing—less advanced than ChatGPT and Gemini.

Best Uses for Grok

1. Getting **real-time social media insights**
2. Understanding **public trends and discussions**
3. Having **casual, humorous AI conversations**

Which AI Chatbot Is Right for You? (Side-by-Side Comparison)

Feature	ChatGPT	DeepSeek	Gemini	Grok
Best For	Writing, brainstorming, learning	Research, factual accuracy	Multimodal (text, images, voice)	Real-time insights, humor
Conversational?	Yes, very natural	No, more factual	Moderate	Yes, more casual
Accuracy	Good, but can make mistakes	High, research-driven	Decent, but sometimes biased	Moderate
Best Use Cases	Writing, coding, general learning	Fact-checking, technical topics	Integrating AI with multimedia	Social media, trending topics

Final Thoughts: The AI Assistant Revolution

AI chatbots **aren't replacing humans**—they're **amplifying human potential.**

Now that you understand how ChatGPT, DeepSeek, Gemini, and Grok work, it's time to explore **how AI can shape your family, career, and education.**

Next up: How AI is making homes, parents, and students smarter than ever!

CHAPTER 3: THE AI-POWERED FUTURE – ARE YOU READY?

The Future Is No Longer a Distant Concept – It's Here

For decades, science fiction painted a future where machines would work alongside humans, helping us solve complex problems, automate daily tasks, and even think creatively. That future isn't **coming—it's already here.**

From **self-driving cars** to **AI-generated music,** from **robot-assisted surgeries** to **personal AI tutors,** the world is **undergoing one of the fastest technological shifts in history.**

But here's the problem: **Most people are still treating AI like it's a novelty.**

They think, *"Oh, AI is cool, but it's not something I need to worry about today."*

That mindset is **dangerous—**because while they hesitate, AI is **rapidly transforming jobs, education, industries, and even the way we think.**

So, here's the big question: **Are you ready for the AI-powered future?**

By the end of this chapter, you'll know:

1. **How AI is shaping the future of work, education, business, and creativity.**

2. **The industries AI is disrupting the most—and how to stay ahead.**
3. **The skills that will matter in an AI-driven world.**
4. **How to future-proof yourself, your family, and your career.**

Let's break it all down.

AI and the Future of Work – What's Changing?

If AI can write, analyze, and even make **decisions**, does that mean **humans will lose their jobs?**

Not exactly. But here's the reality:

AI isn't taking jobs—people who use AI are taking jobs from those who don't.

The biggest shift isn't that AI is replacing humans—it's that **AI is becoming a mandatory tool for workers across every industry.**

Take a look at how AI is reshaping **jobs in different industries:**

Industry	How AI Is Changing It	What It Means for You
Healthcare	AI diagnoses diseases faster than doctors; assists in surgeries	Medical professionals must learn to work alongside AI
Finance	AI-powered fraud detection, robo-advisors for investing	Finance professionals must focus on human judgment & strategy
Education	AI tutors, automated grading, personalized learning	Teachers must learn how to integrate AI into their methods

Marketing	AI analyzes consumer behavior, writes content, runs campaigns	Marketers need to master AI tools for content & ad targeting
Software Development	AI writes and debugs code faster than humans	Programmers need to use AI to enhance productivity

What Jobs Are at Risk?

Any job that involves **repetitive, predictable tasks** is at risk of **automation**.

Jobs that AI is most likely to replace:

1. **Data entry clerks**
2. **Customer support agents** (AI chatbots are replacing human agents)
3. **Retail cashiers** (self-checkout & automated stores)
4. **Basic content writers** (AI tools like ChatGPT generate articles in seconds)

What Jobs Will Thrive in an AI-Driven World?

Jobs that **require creativity, emotional intelligence, and decision-making** are **harder to automate**.

Jobs that AI won't easily replace:

- **AI specialists and engineers** (the people designing AI systems)
- **Doctors & medical professionals** (AI assists but can't replace human judgment)
- **Teachers & educators** (AI tutors are great, but human teachers provide mentorship)
- **Creative professionals** (AI generates ideas, but humans bring originality & vision)

The **bottom line**: AI won't take your job—**someone who knows how to use AI better than you might.**

AI and the Future of Education – The AI Tutor Era

Remember when learning was **just about textbooks and teachers?** Well, **that's over.**

AI is now helping students **learn faster, personalize their education, and get instant feedback.**

How AI is revolutionizing education:

- **AI tutors** give real-time feedback (ChatGPT, Khan Academy AI)
- **AI-powered study guides** personalize learning for each student
- **AI grading systems** reduce workload for teachers

Real-World Example: AI Helping Students

Let's say a student is struggling with **calculus**. Instead of hiring an expensive tutor, they can use an **AI assistant** that:

- **Explains concepts in a way they understand**
- **Generates practice problems and solutions**
- **Adjusts difficulty based on their learning speed**

Example Prompt: *"Explain the chain rule in calculus in simple terms and generate 5 practice problems with step-by-step solutions."*

And just like that, a **student can get personalized help instantly.**

The takeaway? AI isn't replacing teachers—it's making learning smarter.

AI in Business – The New Competitive Advantage

AI isn't just changing **how we work**—it's changing **how businesses operate.**

Companies that use AI are outperforming those that don't.

Here's why:

1. AI analyzes **massive amounts of data** in seconds.
2. AI automates **boring, repetitive tasks**—freeing up human workers for more complex work.
3. AI **predicts customer behavior**, helping businesses make smarter decisions.

Examples of AI in Business

Business Function	How AI Improves It	Example AI Tool
Marketing	AI writes social media posts, ad copy, and blog articles	ChatGPT, Jasper AI
Sales	AI predicts which leads are most likely to convert	Salesforce Einstein
Customer Service	AI chatbots handle FAQs and customer inquiries	Chatbots (Intercom, Zendesk AI)
Finance	AI automates fraud detection and risk analysis	IBM Watson, Kensho

Bottom line? AI isn't replacing businesses—it's making them smarter.

And companies that fail to adopt AI? **They risk getting left behind.**

What Skills Will Matter in an AI-Powered Future?

With AI automating so much, what **skills** will actually matter in the future?

Here are the **top 5 future-proof skills**:

1. **Critical Thinking & Problem-Solving** – AI provides information, but **humans still need to analyze and make decisions.**
2. **Creativity & Innovation** – AI can generate ideas, but **humans bring originality.**
3. **AI Literacy & Prompt Engineering** – Knowing **how to talk to AI effectively** will be a game-changer.
4. **Emotional Intelligence (EQ)** – Leadership, teamwork, and communication **can't be automated.**
5. **Adaptability & Continuous Learning** – AI will **keep evolving**, so people must **keep learning.**

<u>Pro Tip:</u> If you learn how to **use AI tools** effectively, you'll have an **advantage over 90% of the workforce.**

Final Thoughts: The Future Belongs to Those Who Adapt

AI is **not a threat—it's an opportunity.**

It's a tool that can **accelerate careers, improve education, and create better businesses.**

The people who **embrace AI now** will have an **unfair advantage**. Those who ignore it? **They'll struggle to catch up.**

So, ask yourself: **Are you going to watch AI reshape the world from the sidelines—or will you be part of the future?**

Next up: How AI is making homes, parents, and students smarter than ever!

CHAPTER 4: AI FOR THE WHOLE FAMILY – MAKING YOUR HOME SMARTER

Welcome to the AI-Enhanced Home

Imagine a home where:

> ➤ **Your AI assistant** reminds you of your grocery list and even orders items before you run out.
> ➤ **Your kids get instant homework help** with AI-powered tutors that adapt to their learning pace.
> ➤ **AI manages your household budget**, optimizing savings and predicting future expenses.
> ➤ **Your smart home adjusts itself**—lights dim when it's bedtime, the thermostat lowers when no one's home, and security cameras recognize faces to enhance safety.

Sound futuristic? It's already happening. **AI is no longer just for tech geeks—it's becoming an essential tool for modern families.**

If you've ever wished for **more time, less stress, and smarter ways to manage your home and family**, AI might be the answer. In this chapter, we'll explore **how AI is transforming family life—from home automation to education, financial planning, and beyond.**

The Smart Home Revolution – AI in Daily Life

AI-powered smart homes are **no longer just for the ultra-wealthy or tech-savvy**. Today, affordable devices are making homes **smarter, safer, and more efficient.**

AI-Powered Smart Assistants

Virtual assistants like **Amazon Alexa, Google Assistant, and Apple's Siri** have become household staples. But they do **far more than just play music or set reminders**.

Here's how AI assistants are improving daily life:

Task	AI Solution
Grocery shopping	AI analyzes your past purchases and reminds you when to restock
Meal planning	AI suggests recipes based on what's in your fridge
Home security	AI-powered cameras recognize faces and alert you to unknown visitors
Energy efficiency	AI-controlled thermostats adjust temperature based on your schedule
Time management	AI schedules meetings, reminds you of important tasks, and even helps plan vacations

Example: You tell Alexa, *"I'm going on vacation next week."* Your AI assistant:

→ Lowers your thermostat to save energy.
→ Schedules pet feeding reminders for your neighbor.
→ Sends you the weather forecast for your trip.

AI-Powered Home Security

AI-driven security systems are **smarter than traditional alarms.**

Ring, Nest, and Wyze cameras use AI to:

- Recognize **family members vs. strangers.**
- Send **real-time alerts** if suspicious activity is detected.
- Detect **fire or carbon monoxide risks** before they become dangerous.

Pro Tip: AI home security **reduces false alarms**—it knows the difference between a **delivery person and a burglar.**

AI for Parents – Work Smarter, Not Harder

If you're a parent, you already know the **constant juggle** of managing work, kids, finances, and personal time.

AI can't do the laundry (yet), but it can make life easier.

AI for Smarter Financial Planning

Managing a household budget can be overwhelming—but AI can help families **spend smarter and save more.**

Here's how:

Financial Task	AI-Powered Solution
Tracking expenses	AI apps like **Mint and YNAB** analyze spending habits

Saving money	AI tools like **Trim** cancel unused subscriptions
Investing wisely	Robo-advisors like **Wealthfront and Betterment** automate smart investments
Predicting expenses	AI forecasts upcoming bills and suggests ways to cut costs

Example: AI notices you're spending too much on dining out. It suggests:

★ Cutting back by **25% to save $200/month.**
★ Sending you easy **at-home meal prep recipes**.

AI for Time Management & Organization

AI isn't just about **saving money**—it also helps parents save **time**.

Best AI Productivity Tools for Parents:

- **Google Calendar AI** – Schedules your work meetings **around** your child's school events.
- **Todoist AI** – Creates **personalized to-do lists** based on your daily routine.
- **Notion AI** – Helps you **organize family schedules, travel plans, and meal prep** in one place.

Pro Tip: Ask ChatGPT, *"Create a morning routine checklist for my 10-year-old to get ready for school faster."*

AI for Kids – Learning, Playing, and Growing Smarter

Your child is growing up in an **AI-driven world**—so why not let AI **help them learn smarter?**

AI-Powered Learning Assistants

Instead of struggling with tough subjects, students can now use **AI tutors** for **instant help**.

Best AI Learning Tools for Kids:

Subject	AI-Powered Learning Tool	How It Helps
Math	ChatGPT, Photomath	Solves equations step by step
Science	Wolfram Alpha	Explains physics & chemistry concepts
Reading	Google's Read Along	Uses AI to teach pronunciation
Languages	Duolingo AI	Adaptive language lessons

Example: A student struggling with algebra can ask:

→ *"Explain quadratic equations like I'm 10 years old."*
→ *"Generate 5 practice problems with step-by-step solutions."*

And in seconds, AI **personalizes learning** for them.

AI for Homework & SAT Prep

AI doesn't just help with **daily schoolwork**—it's also a game-changer for **SAT, ACT, and AP test prep**.

How AI Helps with Exam Prep:

→ AI generates **custom practice tests** based on **previous SAT/ACT exams**.
→ AI breaks down **complex essay prompts** into easy-to-follow outlines.

➔ AI-powered flashcards help students **memorize key facts quickly**.

Example Prompt for SAT Prep:

➔ *"Create a 10-question SAT math quiz with answer explanations."*

AI and Family Bonding – Yes, Even Fun Can Be Smart!

AI isn't just for **work and school**—it can also **bring families together**.

Fun AI-Powered Activities for Families:

★ AI-powered **storytelling apps** – Turn bedtime stories into interactive adventures.

★ AI **recipe generators** – Plan creative family dinners with surprise ingredients.

★ AI **music & games** – AI-generated music apps let kids compose their own songs.

Pro Tip: Ask ChatGPT, *"Create a funny bedtime story about a robot and a dinosaur."*

Final Thoughts: Embracing AI in Family Life

The future **isn't about AI replacing families**—it's about AI **helping families thrive**.

Key Takeaways from This Chapter:

➔ AI-powered smart homes **save time, money, and stress**.

➔ Parents can use AI to **manage schedules, finances, and work-life balance**.

➔ AI helps kids **learn smarter and prepare for future careers**.

➔ AI even makes **family fun more creative and interactive**.

So, the question is: **How will you use AI to make your home smarter?**

Next up: How AI is helping kids and students master school subjects with ease!

CHAPTER 5: AI FOR KIDS & STUDENTS – THE FUTURE OF LEARNING

A New Era of Education – Learning with AI

Education is changing faster than ever before. The old-school method of memorizing textbooks and sitting through **one-size-fits-all lessons** is being replaced by something **far smarter, more personalized, and engaging**—AI-powered learning.

If you're a student (or a parent of one), imagine this:

→ **A personal AI tutor** that explains math problems step by step.
→ **Instant answers to science questions**, without endless Googling.
→ **Practice tests generated on demand** to prepare for exams.
→ **AI-powered language tutors** that help with Spanish, French, or any language.

Sounds futuristic? **It's already happening.**

AI is turning learning into something **customized, interactive, and available anytime, anywhere.**

In this chapter, we'll explore:

➤ How AI is transforming education—from elementary school to college.

➤ The best AI tools for learning math, science, and languages.

➤ How AI is helping students prepare for SATs, ACTs, and other exams.

➤ How students can use AI ethically and avoid common pitfalls.

The Old Way vs. The AI-Powered Way of Learning

For decades, education has been stuck in the same model:
Teachers lecture → Students take notes → Memorize for tests.

But this method has serious flaws:

➔ **One teacher for 30+ students** means **not everyone gets personalized help.**

➔ **Students learn at different speeds,** but schools move at one fixed pace.

➔ **Traditional learning lacks interactivity,** making it hard to stay engaged.

AI changes all of that.

With AI-powered tutors, **students get instant, customized explanations** tailored to their learning style.

The AI-Powered Way of Learning

➔ **Students learn at their own pace** – AI adjusts based on their progress.

➔ **Interactive learning** – AI uses quizzes, videos, and even games to teach.

➔ **Instant feedback** – AI tells students *exactly* what they got wrong and how to fix it.

Example:

➔ If a student struggles with **algebra**, AI can:

➔ Identify what concepts they don't understand.

→ Generate **practice problems** at their skill level.

→ Provide **step-by-step solutions** with explanations.

The takeaway? AI isn't replacing teachers—it's making learning smarter and more personalized.

AI Tools That Help Students Learn Smarter

AI is **already in classrooms and homes,** helping students with **everything from math to history to essay writing.**

Here are some of the **top AI-powered learning tools** students can use today:

Subject	AI-Powered Learning Tool	How It Helps
Math	**Photomath, Wolfram Alpha**	Solves problems step by step, provides explanations
Science	**Google Bard, Khan Academy AI**	Explains concepts like physics & chemistry
Writing	**Grammarly, ChatGPT**	Helps with essays, grammar, and sentence structure
Languages	**Duolingo AI, ChatGPT**	Personalized language learning & real-time translations
History & Social Studies	**Perplexity AI, ChatGPT**	Summarizes historical events and key concepts

Example Prompt:

➔ *"Explain Newton's laws of motion in simple terms with examples."*

With one click, AI **transforms complex ideas into easy-to-understand lessons.**

AI for Math & Science – The Ultimate Homework Helper

Math and science can be **some of the toughest subjects**—but AI makes them easier.

AI-Powered Math Assistance

- **Photomath** – Students snap a photo of a math problem, and AI **solves it step by step.**
- **Wolfram Alpha** – A powerful AI calculator that **explains the "why" behind every answer.**
- **ChatGPT & Gemini** – Can **generate math practice problems** and solutions.

Example:

➔ *"Solve this quadratic equation: $x^2 - 5x + 6 = 0$, and explain it in simple terms."*

AI for Science Learning

- AI **simulates experiments** (great for chemistry and physics).
- AI can **generate science quizzes** to test knowledge.
- AI can **explain difficult concepts** with real-world examples.

Example:

➔ *"Describe how photosynthesis works like a factory assembly line."*

The result? AI turns abstract concepts into **fun, relatable, and understandable lessons.**

Using AI for Exam Preparation (SAT, ACT, & More!)

Standardized tests like the **SAT, ACT, and AP exams** are crucial for college admissions. AI can help students **study smarter—not harder.**

How AI Helps with Exam Prep

- **Generates SAT/ACT practice questions** based on previous exams.
- **Explains wrong answers** so students can learn from mistakes.
- **Creates personalized study plans** to improve weak areas.

Example Prompt for SAT Prep:

➔ *"Generate 10 SAT-style math questions with answer explanations."*

Example Prompt for Writing:

➔ *"Give me feedback on this SAT essay and suggest improvements."*

AI **adapts to each student,** making sure they get **targeted, personalized prep.**

The result? Better scores with less stress.

AI in Language Learning – Your Personal AI Language Tutor

Learning a new language? AI can help with:

1. **Pronunciation practice** (AI corrects mistakes instantly).
2. **Grammar and vocabulary quizzes** (customized to skill level).
3. **Conversational practice** (AI acts like a virtual speaking partner).

Best AI Language Tools:

1. **Duolingo AI** – AI-powered lessons that adapt to your learning pace.
2. **ChatGPT / Gemini** – AI chats with you in different languages.
3. **Google Translate AI** – Real-time translations and speech recognition.

Example Prompt:

➜ *"Help me practice ordering food in a restaurant in Spanish."*

The **result? AI makes language learning more immersive and engaging.**

Using AI Ethically – The Do's & Don'ts for Students

AI is a **powerful tool**—but it should be used **responsibly.**

How to Use AI the Right Way

➜ **Use AI for explanations, not just answers.**
➜ **Generate practice problems** and solve them yourself.
➜ **Get feedback on essays**, but do the writing yourself.

Common AI Mistakes to Avoid

1. Copying AI-generated essays and submitting them as your own.
2. Using AI for test answers instead of learning the material.
3. Relying too much on AI and not thinking critically.

The best way to use AI?

Let it guide you—but don't let it do everything for you.

Final Thoughts: The Future of Learning with AI

Key Takeaways from This Chapter:

1. AI is **revolutionizing education**, making learning **faster and more interactive.**
2. AI-powered tutors help students **with math, science, writing, and languages.**
3. AI can **generate practice tests** for SAT, ACT, and AP exams.
4. **Ethical AI use** ensures students actually learn, not just copy answers.

The future of learning is here—so why not use AI to get ahead?

Next up: How parents can use AI to make life easier and help guide their family's future!

CHAPTER 6: AI FOR PARENTS – HOW TO STAY AHEAD & GUIDE YOUR FAMILY

Why Parents Need to Embrace AI Now

Parenting has always been challenging, but **the AI revolution is adding a new layer of complexity**. The world our children are growing up in **isn't the same as the one we knew**—education, careers, and everyday life are all being reshaped by artificial intelligence.

As a parent, you might be asking:

1. **How do I prepare my kids for a future where AI is everywhere?**
2. **How can I use AI to make parenting easier and more efficient?**
3. **What AI skills do I need to learn so I don't fall behind?**

Here's the reality: Ignoring AI is no longer an option.

This chapter will show you how to **stay ahead, make smarter parenting decisions,** and **ensure your family thrives in an AI-driven world.**

How AI Can Help Parents Save Time and Reduce Stress

Between work, school, activities, and household responsibilities, modern parenting often feels **like juggling a hundred tasks at once**. AI can't replace parents, but it **can take care of some of the mental load** and help families function more smoothly.

AI for Managing Family Schedules

AI-powered tools help parents **stay organized and keep track of daily tasks**.

Best AI Productivity Tools for Parents:

Task	AI-Powered Solution
Managing schedules	Google Calendar AI, TimeHero
Setting reminders	Alexa, Google Assistant
Organizing to-do lists	Todoist AI, Notion AI
Automating chores	Smart home assistants

Example:

→ Ask ChatGPT: *"Create a weekly schedule for my family, including work, school, sports, and meal prep."*

The result? AI helps parents get more organized with less effort.

AI for Smarter Decision-Making as a Parent

Every day, parents make **hundreds of decisions**—from what to cook for dinner to how to help their child with school struggles.

AI can help by:

→ Providing instant, research-backed parenting advice.

→ Analyzing trends in children's education and mental health.

→ Offering personalized recommendations based on your family's needs.

How AI Can Help Parents Make Better Decisions:

- **Health & Nutrition** – AI meal planners suggest balanced diets for kids.
- **Education** – AI-powered tutors help children with homework.
- **Screen Time Management** – AI suggests age-appropriate content for kids.

Example:

→ Ask ChatGPT: *"What are healthy snack ideas for a 10-year-old with food allergies?"*

The result? **AI provides quick, tailored parenting advice.**

AI for Financial Planning & Budgeting

Raising a family is expensive—but **AI can help parents make smarter financial decisions.**

AI-Powered Budgeting & Saving

AI apps analyze spending habits and help families **save money**.

Best AI Financial Tools for Families:

Financial Task	AI-Powered Tool
Tracking expenses	Mint, YNAB
Cutting unnecessary spending	Trim AI

Smart investing	Betterment, Wealthfront
Planning for college	AI-powered financial advisors

Example:

➤ AI notices you **spend $300/month on takeout** and suggests:
  ○ Reducing it to **$150/month**, saving $1,800 per year.
  ○ Providing **easy home-cooked meal ideas** to replace takeout.

The result? AI helps parents build a smarter financial future.

Preparing Your Kids for an AI-Driven Future

The biggest gift you can give your kids is **preparing them for the future**—and AI will be a major part of that.

What Every Parent Should Teach Their Kids About AI

1. **AI is a tool, not a replacement for thinking.**
2. **AI-powered careers will be in high demand.**
3. **Understanding AI now will give kids a competitive edge.**

Pro Tip: Parents don't need to be AI experts—**just learning the basics helps guide your kids better.**

AI for Home Life – Making Parenting Easier

AI-powered smart homes **help reduce daily stress** by automating simple tasks.

Best AI Smart Home Tools for Families:

- ★ **AI-powered security systems** (Ring, Nest).
- ★ **Smart thermostats** that adjust temperature automatically.
- ★ **AI shopping assistants** that reorder household items before they run out.

Example:

- → Your smart fridge notices **milk is low** and **automatically adds it to your grocery list.**

The result? AI makes everyday parenting tasks easier.

Ethical AI Use – Teaching Kids to Use AI Responsibly

AI is a **powerful tool**, but kids must **learn to use it wisely.**

What Parents Should Teach Kids About AI

1. **AI can be helpful, but always fact-check information.**
2. **Don't rely on AI to do homework—use it to learn.**
3. **Be aware of privacy risks when using AI tools.**

AI Mistakes Kids Should Avoid

1. **Using AI to cheat on school assignments.**
2. **Sharing personal information with AI chatbots.**
3. **Believing everything AI-generated without verifying facts.**

The takeaway? Parents should guide kids to use AI ethically and responsibly.

Final Thoughts: AI is a Parent's Secret Weapon

Key Takeaways from This Chapter:

→ AI helps parents **stay organized and manage busy schedules.**

→ AI makes **smarter financial planning and budgeting easier.**

→ AI-powered learning tools **prepare kids for an AI-driven future.**

→ Parents should **teach kids how to use AI responsibly.**

The bottom line? **AI** won't replace parents—it will make parenting smarter.

Next up: How kids can use **AI** to master math, science, and school subjects!

CHAPTER 7: LEARNING MATH & SCIENCE USING PROMPT ENGINEERING

How AI is Changing the Way We Learn Math & Science

For years, students have struggled with math and science. Concepts like **algebra, calculus, physics, and chemistry** can feel overwhelming.

But what if you had a **personal AI tutor** available 24/7? One that explains things step by step, **creates custom practice problems, and adapts to your learning style?**

That's exactly what **AI and prompt engineering** can do.

What You'll Learn in This Chapter:

> ➢ What is prompt engineering, and why does it matter?
> ➢ How AI can generate math and science explanations, practice problems, and step-by-step solutions.
> ➢ How students can prepare for standardized tests (SAT, ACT) using AI.
> ➢ How families can use AI to learn almost anything—math, science, history, and more.

By the end of this chapter, you'll know **how to use AI to make learning easier, smarter, and more engaging.**

What is Prompt Engineering? (And Why Does It Matter?)

Understanding AI Prompting

When you ask a chatbot like ChatGPT a question, you're giving it a **prompt**.

But **not all prompts are equal.**

Example:

- **Bad Prompt:** *"Explain calculus."*
- **Good Prompt:** *"Explain the concept of derivatives in calculus in simple terms with real-world examples."*

Prompt engineering is the skill of asking AI the **right questions** to get the most useful answers.

AI for Math – Step-by-Step Problem Solving

Math can be tough, but AI **can break down problems like a personal tutor.**

How AI Helps with Math

- ➤ **Step-by-step explanations** – AI walks through problems **like a teacher would.**
- ➤ **Custom-generated practice problems** – AI creates **problems tailored to your level.**
- ➤ **Instant feedback** – AI **tells you where you made mistakes and how to fix them.**

Example Prompt for Algebra:

- ➔ *"Explain how to factor quadratic equations with three examples and solutions."*

Example Prompt for Geometry:

➔ *"Generate 5 practice problems on calculating the area of triangles, with step-by-step solutions."*

AI helps students understand difficult math topics faster and more effectively.

AI for Science – Making Complex Topics Simple

Science is full of abstract concepts, but AI **can make them engaging and easy to understand.**

How AI Helps with Science

➔ **Breaks down difficult topics** – AI explains physics, chemistry, and biology in simple terms.
➔ **Creates science experiments** – AI suggests hands-on experiments for students.
➔ **Generates quizzes** – AI creates personalized quizzes to reinforce learning.

Example Prompt for Physics:

➔ *"Explain Newton's three laws of motion with real-world examples."*

Example Prompt for Chemistry:

➔ *"Describe the periodic table and its elements in a way a 10-year-old can understand."*

AI turns science into an interactive learning experience.

Preparing for the SAT & ACT with AI

Standardized tests like the **SAT and ACT** require serious preparation. AI **can create customized study plans, generate practice tests, and offer real-time feedback.**

AI-Powered Exam Prep

→ **AI generates SAT/ACT-style questions** tailored to the student's level
→ **AI breaks down essay prompts** and suggests strong arguments.
→ **AI tracks weak areas** and recommends extra practice.

Example Prompt for SAT Math Prep:

→ *"Generate a 10-question SAT math quiz with answer explanations."*

Example Prompt for SAT Reading Prep:

→ *"Summarize this reading passage and generate three comprehension questions."*

With AI, students can prepare smarter, not harder.

Using AI to Learn Almost Anything

AI isn't just for math and science—it can **help families learn any subject.**

How AI Can Help Families Learn Together

→ **History & Geography** – AI summarizes key historical events.
→ **Foreign Languages** – AI tutors help with pronunciation and grammar.
→ **Creative Writing** – AI gives feedback on essays and stories.

Example Prompt for History:

→ *"Summarize the causes and effects of World War II in 5 key points."*

Example Prompt for Language Learning:

➔ *"Teach me 10 common phrases in French for traveling."*

AI makes learning fun and accessible for the whole family.

Final Thoughts: AI as the Ultimate Learning Partner

Key Takeaways from This Chapter:

➔ Prompt engineering helps students get the best answers from AI.

➔ AI makes math and science learning more interactive and personalized.

➔ AI helps students prepare for standardized tests like the SAT & ACT.

➔ AI can help families learn almost anything—history, languages, and beyond.

The bottom line? AI can make learning easier, smarter, and even more fun.

Next up: How AI is helping families learn coding, IT skills, and even automate daily tasks!

CHAPTER 8: LEARN CODING & IT SKILLS USING AI – AUTOMATE & GET SMARTER

Why Learning to Code Matters More Than Ever

Once upon a time, **coding was a niche skill**—only necessary for computer scientists and software engineers. But in an AI-driven world, **understanding how technology works is just as essential as knowing how to read and write.**

Why Everyone (Including Kids & Parents) Should Learn Coding:

→ AI is creating more tech-driven jobs than ever before.
→ Understanding coding helps you work better with AI.
→ Even basic coding skills give you an edge in almost any career.

But here's the exciting part: **AI is making coding easier to learn than ever before.**

Whether you're a complete beginner or a professional looking to expand your skills, AI-powered coding tools **can guide you step by step**—making programming more **accessible, interactive, and fun.**

In this chapter, we'll explore:

→ How AI can teach coding to beginners and kids.

→ How AI helps software developers code faster and smarter.

→ How families can use AI for home automation and daily tasks.

By the end, you'll know how to **leverage AI to master coding and IT skills for the future.**

How AI is Revolutionizing Coding Education

In the past, learning to code meant **reading textbooks or watching long tutorials**—which could feel overwhelming.

AI changes everything by:

1. **Providing real-time explanations.**
2. **Generating sample code instantly.**
3. **Helping debug errors step by step.**

The takeaway? With AI, anyone can start coding—without prior experience.

AI Tools That Teach Coding & Programming

There are now AI-powered platforms that **teach coding in a simple, interactive way.**

Best AI Tools for Learning to Code:

Tool	Best For	How It Helps
ChatGPT (Code Interpreter Mode)	Beginners & professionals	Generates and explains code
GitHub Copilot	Developers	Suggests and auto-completes code

Code.org AI Lab	Kids & beginners	Teaches basic programming concepts interactively
Replit AI	Web developers	Helps debug and write scripts in multiple languages
Khan Academy AI	Students & self-learners	Step-by-step coding lessons

Example Prompt for Learning Python:

→ *"Teach me Python basics with a simple step-by-step project."*

Example Prompt for Debugging Code:

→ *"Here's my code—it's not working. Can you help me find the error?"*

AI acts like a personal tutor—guiding you through coding problems and projects.

How AI Helps Software Developers Work Faster

If you're a **developer**, AI is the **ultimate productivity booster.**

AI for Debugging & Code Optimization

AI can:

1. **Find and fix bugs instantly.**
2. **Suggest more efficient ways to write code.**
3. **Auto-generate code snippets based on project requirements.**

Example Prompt for Debugging JavaScript:

→ *"My JavaScript function isn't running correctly—can you debug it?"*

The result? Faster coding, fewer errors, and higher efficiency.

Using AI to Automate Tasks at Home

AI isn't just for **learning to code**—it can also **automate daily tasks**, making home life more efficient.

How AI Can Automate Household Tasks:

➔ **Automating emails & reminders** – AI schedules meetings, replies to messages.
➔ **Managing finances** – AI tracks expenses and suggests smart spending habits.
➔ **Home automation** – AI-powered devices adjust lights, control temperature, and secure your home.

Example Prompt for Home Automation:

➔ *"Write a simple Python script to turn my smart lights on at sunset."*

The takeaway? AI-powered coding isn't just for professionals—it can improve daily life.

Final Thoughts: AI Makes Coding Easier & More Useful Than Ever

Key Takeaways from This Chapter:

1. AI-powered coding assistants **make learning programming accessible to everyone.**
2. Developers can use AI to **debug, write, and optimize code faster.**
3. AI can automate **daily tasks, making life easier for families.**
4. Even basic coding skills **give you an edge in an AI-powered world.**

The bottom line? AI isn't just changing how we work—it's changing how we learn and interact with technology.

Next up: How AI can help you make smarter decisions in work, business, and life!

CHAPTER 9: HOW AI CAN HELP YOU MAKE SMARTER DECISIONS

The Power of AI in Decision-Making

Every day, we make **hundreds of decisions**—some small, like choosing what to eat for dinner, and some life-changing, like deciding on a career move or an investment.

But what if **you had an assistant that could analyze vast amounts of data, predict outcomes, and provide the best possible recommendations**?

That's exactly what **AI-powered decision-making tools** can do.

How AI Helps Us Make Smarter Choices:

→ Analyzes data faster than humans ever could.
→ Reduces emotional bias and focuses on facts.
→ Identifies patterns and trends we might miss.
→ Helps make better financial, career, and life decisions.

The takeaway? AI isn't here to replace human judgment—it's here to enhance it.

AI for Financial Decision-Making – Managing Money Smarter

Money is one of the most important areas where **AI-driven decision-making** can make a huge impact.

AI for Budgeting & Expense Tracking

AI can analyze **your spending habits** and suggest ways to **save money**.

Best AI-Powered Financial Tools:

Task	AI-Powered Tool
Tracking expenses	Mint, YNAB
Investing smarter	Betterment, Wealthfront
Finding & canceling unused subscriptions	Trim AI
Predicting future expenses	Cleo AI

Example Prompt:

➔ *"Analyze my monthly expenses and suggest where I can save money."*

The result? AI helps you make smarter financial decisions, with less effort.

AI for Career Growth & Job Market Predictions

Careers are evolving **faster than ever**—so how do you stay ahead?

How AI Helps with Career Decisions:

→ **AI-powered job matching** – Finds the best job opportunities based on your skills.

→ **Resume optimization** – AI tools like ChatGPT rewrite resumes for better impact.

→ **Predicts in-demand skills** – AI identifies future job trends so you can upskill.

Example Prompt:

→ *"What skills should I learn in the next five years to stay competitive in the job market?"*

The result? AI gives you career insights based on real-world data, not just guesswork.

AI for Smarter Investments & Business Decisions

Investing and business strategy require **analyzing vast amounts of data**—something AI excels at.

How AI Helps with Investing & Business:

→ **Analyzes stock market trends** to predict potential investments.

→ **Optimizes pricing strategies** for businesses.

→ **Identifies fraud and financial risks.**

Example Prompt for Business Owners:

→ *"Analyze customer feedback from my online store and suggest improvements."*

The takeaway? AI helps businesses and investors make data-driven choices.

AI for Personal Life & Health Decisions

AI isn't just about **money and careers**—it can help you make smarter **daily life choices** too.

AI-Powered Decision-Making for Personal Life:

➔ **AI-powered meal planning** – Suggests healthy meals based on diet preferences.
➔ **AI fitness coaching** – Creates personalized workout plans.
➔ **AI-powered mental health assistants** – Tools like Woebot help with stress management.

Example Prompt:

➔ *"Create a weekly meal plan for a healthy diet based on my food preferences."*

The result? AI makes managing personal well-being easier and smarter.

Final Thoughts: Smarter Decisions with AI

Key Takeaways from This Chapter:

1. AI helps with **financial, career, investment, and personal life decisions.**
2. AI **reduces human bias** by focusing on data and logic.
3. AI helps **business owners, job seekers, and families plan for the future.**
4. AI is **not a replacement for human thinking—it's a tool for better decision-making.**

The bottom line? AI makes smarter decisions faster—but you still control the final choice.

Next up: How businesses and entrepreneurs can use AI to stay ahead!

CHAPTER 10: AI & BUSINESS – HOW TO USE AI FOR SUCCESS

AI Is Reshaping Business – Are You Ready?

AI isn't just a tool—it's a **business revolution**. From **startups to Fortune 500 companies**, AI is changing the way businesses **analyze data, interact with customers, market products, and even make financial decisions.**

Why AI is a Game-Changer for Business:

→ **Automates repetitive tasks**, freeing up time for strategy and growth.
→ **Analyzes customer behavior**, helping businesses tailor products and services.
→ **Boosts marketing effectiveness**, optimizing ads and content in real-time.
→ **Reduces costs and increases efficiency**, making businesses more competitive.

The businesses that **adopt AI now** will have a massive advantage. The ones that **ignore it?** They risk being left behind.

In this chapter, we'll explore:

1. **How AI is transforming different business functions (marketing, sales, HR, finance, operations).**

2. **The best AI tools for business owners, entrepreneurs, and freelancers.**
3. **How small businesses can use AI to compete with big corporations.**

By the end, you'll know **how to use AI to make your business smarter, faster, and more profitable.**

AI in Marketing – Smarter Ads, Content & Customer Engagement

Marketing has always been about **understanding customers**—but AI makes it possible to analyze **millions of data points in seconds** to create **highly targeted, effective campaigns.**

How AI is Changing Marketing:

★ **AI-generated content** – Writes blogs, social media posts, and product descriptions.
★ **Smart ad targeting** – AI analyzes **who is most likely to buy and targets ads accordingly.**
★ **Customer sentiment analysis** – AI tools scan **social media and reviews** to understand public perception.

Best AI Marketing Tools:

Marketing Task	AI-Powered Tool
Writing blog posts & ads	Jasper AI, Copy.ai
SEO optimization	Surfer SEO, Clearscope
Social media management	Lately AI, Predis AI

Ad targeting & analytics	Facebook AI, Google Ads AI

Example Prompt:

➔ *"Write a compelling Facebook ad for a new eco-friendly water bottle."*

The result? AI makes marketing more effective, personalized, and data-driven.

AI in Sales – Closing More Deals, Faster

AI is **revolutionizing sales** by helping businesses:

1. **Predict which leads are most likely to convert.**
2. **Automate follow-up emails and responses.**
3. **Analyze past sales data to refine strategies.**

Best AI Sales Tools:

Sales Task	AI-Powered Tool
Lead generation	HubSpot AI, Apollo AI
Sales forecasting	Gong AI, Salesforce Einstein
Automated email follow-ups	Reply.io, Smartlead AI
Chatbots for customer engagement	Drift, Intercom AI

Example Prompt:

➔ *"Analyze my past sales data and suggest ways to improve conversion rates."*

The result? AI helps businesses **sell smarter and close more deals faster.**

AI in Finance – Smarter Spending & Risk Management

Financial decision-making is **complex**, but AI can **process data at incredible speeds** to:

→ Detect fraud and suspicious activity.
→ Automate budgeting and cost-cutting strategies.
→ Help businesses make better investment decisions.

Best AI Financial Tools:

Finance Task	AI-Powered Tool
Expense tracking	QuickBooks AI, Ramp
Fraud detection	FICO AI, Feedzai
Automated bookkeeping	Xero AI, Zoho Books
Investment analysis	Kensho AI, Bloomberg AI

Example Prompt:

→ *"Analyze my business expenses and suggest areas where I can save money."*

The result? AI makes financial decision-making **faster, smarter, and more secure.**

AI in HR – Hiring the Right People, Faster

Hiring and managing employees is **one of the biggest challenges** for any business. AI helps by:

→ **Automating resume screening and applicant tracking.**
→ **Predicting which candidates will perform best in a role.**

➔ Helping businesses retain top talent by analyzing employee engagement.

Best AI HR Tools:

HR Task	AI-Powered Tool
Resume screening	Pymetrics AI, HireVue
Employee engagement analysis	Peakon AI, Workday AI
Automated onboarding	Rippling AI, BambooHR
Performance tracking	Lattice AI, 15Five AI

Example Prompt:

➔ *"Analyze these 50 resumes and shortlist the top 5 candidates for a marketing manager role."*

The result? AI helps businesses **hire smarter and retain top talent.**

AI for Small Businesses – Leveling the Playing Field

Many small business owners worry that **AI is only for big companies**—but the truth is, AI is making it easier than ever for **small businesses to compete.**

How Small Businesses Can Use AI:

1. **Chatbots** – Automate customer service **without hiring extra staff.**

2. **AI-generated social media content** – Saves **time and money on marketing.**
3. **Smart financial tools** – Help **manage budgets and maximize profits.**

Example Prompt for a Small Business Owner:

➔ *"Generate a 5-day social media content plan for my online clothing store."*

The takeaway? AI levels the playing field, making small businesses more competitive.

The Future of AI in Business – What's Coming Next?

AI **isn't slowing down**—it's just getting started.

Future AI Business Trends:

➔ **AI-powered virtual assistants** – AI that handles **entire business processes automatically.**
➔ **Advanced AI personalization** – Products and ads that **adapt to individual users in real time.**
➔ **AI-powered creativity** – AI that generates **videos, music, and even product designs.**

Pro Tip: Businesses that **start using AI now** will **stay ahead of the competition.**

Final Thoughts: AI is the New Competitive Advantage

Key Takeaways from This Chapter:

1. AI **automates marketing, sales, finance, and HR** to boost efficiency.

2. AI helps **businesses grow faster and stay competitive.**
3. AI is **not just for big companies—small businesses can use it too.**
4. The future of AI in business **is limitless—and those who adopt it early will win.**

The bottom line? AI is the future of business success.

Next up: Understanding AI ethics, risks, and how to use AI responsibly.

CHAPTER 11: AI, ETHICS & RISKS – THE OTHER SIDE OF THE COIN

AI: A Double-Edged Sword

AI is a powerful tool that is transforming **business, education, healthcare, and daily life**. But like any major technological advancement, **it comes with risks and ethical dilemmas.**

While AI has the potential to **increase productivity, automate tedious tasks, and enhance decision-making**, it also raises **critical questions about privacy, bias, misinformation, and job displacement.**

Why AI Ethics & Risks Matter:

- → **AI can reinforce human biases** if not carefully monitored.
- → **Privacy concerns** arise with AI analyzing vast amounts of personal data.
- → **Misinformation & deepfakes** can manipulate public perception.
- → **Job displacement** is a real concern in certain industries.

The future of AI isn't just about **how powerful it becomes—**it's about **how responsibly we use it.**

In this chapter, we'll explore:

1. The biggest ethical challenges AI presents.
2. How AI bias happens—and how to reduce it.
3. The risks of AI in privacy, misinformation, and security.
4. How businesses and individuals can use AI responsibly.

AI & Bias – Can Machines Be Fair?

One of the biggest concerns with AI is **bias**—the idea that AI systems can make **unfair or prejudiced decisions**. But how does this happen?

How AI Bias Occurs

AI is trained on **massive datasets collected from the internet, books, and human-written content**. If the data contains **biases**, AI models can **unintentionally learn and repeat them**.

Real-World Examples of AI Bias:

➜ **Hiring discrimination** – AI resume-screening tools **favor certain candidates over others** based on biased training data.
➜ **Racial bias in facial recognition** – Some AI-powered facial recognition tools **misidentify people of color at higher rates**.
➜ **Gender bias in job ads** – AI-driven advertising platforms **sometimes show high-paying job ads more often to men than women**.

Example:

➜ In 2018, Amazon scrapped an AI-powered hiring tool because it **showed bias against women** in tech job applications.

How to Reduce AI Bias:

1. **Train AI on diverse datasets** to reduce bias.
2. **Regularly audit AI decision-making** to identify unfair patterns.
3. **Include human oversight** in AI-driven hiring, lending, and healthcare decisions.

The takeaway? AI isn't naturally fair—it learns from human data, so we must guide it carefully.

AI & Privacy – Who Controls Your Data?

Every time we use AI-powered apps—**whether it's ChatGPT, Google Assistant, or facial recognition software**—we're sharing **personal data**.

This raises important **privacy questions**:

1. **Who owns the data AI collects?**
2. **How is our information being used?**
3. **Can AI be hacked or misused for surveillance?**

The Privacy Risks of AI

★ **AI chatbots store conversations** – Some companies use AI-generated data for **training future models**.
★ **Facial recognition & surveillance** – AI-powered cameras track people in public spaces.
★ **Smart home devices listen constantly** – Virtual assistants like Alexa & Google Home collect voice data.

How to Protect Your Privacy with AI:

1. **Use AI tools that prioritize privacy** (e.g., encrypted AI assistants).
2. **Turn off data tracking settings** on smart devices.
3. **Be mindful of what personal information you share with AI tools.**

Example:

➔ OpenAI faced backlash when users discovered **ChatGPT conversations were stored and analyzed** for improving future responses.

The takeaway? **AI privacy concerns are real, but you can take steps to protect yourself.**

AI & Misinformation – Can We Trust What AI Generates?

AI is incredibly powerful at **creating content**—but that also means it can be used to **spread misinformation.**

Examples of AI-Generated Misinformation:

➔ **Fake news articles** – AI can generate **convincing but false stories** that spread quickly.
➔ **Deepfake videos** – AI creates **realistic-looking videos of people saying things they never said.**
➔ **False academic papers** – AI-generated research papers have **fooled real scientists.**

Example:

· ➔ In 2023, a deepfake video of a world leader **went viral, causing panic before it was debunked.**

How to Spot AI Misinformation

➔ **Check sources** – If an article sounds suspicious, verify it with **trusted news sources.**
➔ **Look for signs of AI-generated images** – Many deepfakes have **unnatural eye movement and odd details.**
➔ **Use AI detection tools** – Platforms like **Deepware and Sensity AI** help identify deepfakes.

The takeaway? AI can create convincing misinformation—so always verify before believing or sharing content.

AI & Job Displacement – What Jobs Are at Risk?

Many people worry that **AI will take their jobs**—and in some cases, that concern is valid.

Jobs Most at Risk of AI Displacement:

1. **Data entry & clerical work** – AI automates **repetitive office tasks.**
2. **Customer service** – AI chatbots are **handling more support requests.**
3. **Basic writing & translation** – AI-generated content **reduces the need for human writers in some areas.**

Jobs AI Can't Easily Replace

1. **Creative jobs** – AI can generate content, but humans **bring originality and vision.**
2. **Skilled trades** – Electricians, plumbers, and mechanics **require hands-on expertise.**
3. **Emotional intelligence roles** – Therapists, nurses, and teachers **rely on human connection.**

Example Prompt:

→ *"What skills should I learn to stay relevant in an AI-driven job market?"*

The takeaway? AI won't replace jobs—it will change them. The key is to **adapt and upskill.**

How to Use AI Responsibly – The Do's & Don'ts

How to Use AI Ethically

1. Use AI to enhance work, not replace human expertise.
2. Ensure AI-generated content is fact-checked before sharing.
3. Advocate for transparency in AI decision-making.

AI Ethical Pitfalls to Avoid

1. Using AI to spread misinformation or manipulate people.
2. Letting AI replace human judgment in critical decisions.
3. Relying on AI without verifying its recommendations.

Pro Tip: Businesses and individuals should adopt **"ethical AI usage policies"** to ensure AI is used responsibly.

Final Thoughts: The AI Future is in Our Hands

Key Takeaways from This Chapter:

1. AI can be biased, but **we can reduce bias with better training and oversight.**
2. AI raises privacy concerns, but **users can take steps to protect their data.**
3. AI-generated misinformation is a real threat—**always verify content before trusting it.**
4. AI will change the job market—**but those who adapt and learn AI skills will stay ahead.**
5. **Ethical AI usage is a responsibility we all share.**

The bottom line? AI is neither good nor bad—it depends on how we use it.

Next up: The final chapter—How to ride the AI wave and future-proof yourself!

CHAPTER 12: THE FUTURE IS NOW – HOW TO RIDE THE AI WAVE

AI Isn't Waiting – Are You Ready to Take Advantage of It?

The AI revolution isn't coming—it's **already here.**

Every industry, every job, every aspect of life is being reshaped by artificial intelligence. **The question isn't whether AI will impact you—it's whether you'll be ready for it.**

Why Embracing AI Now is Critical:

- ★ **AI is accelerating faster than any previous technology.**
- ★ **Those who learn how to use AI will have a massive advantage.**
- ★ **Ignoring AI means falling behind in careers, education, and business.**

But here's the good news: **It's not too late to get started.**

This chapter is your **AI action plan**—practical steps you can take **right now** to learn AI, apply it in your daily life, and future-proof yourself for the AI-powered world.

Step 1: Start Using AI Every Day

The best way to **understand AI** is to **start using it.**

Simple AI-Powered Tasks You Can Do Today:

- → **Ask ChatGPT** to summarize a complex topic.
- → **Use AI for productivity** (automate emails, schedule meetings).
- → **Explore AI-powered tools** for writing, coding, or business analytics.
- → **Test an AI tutor** (for learning math, languages, or any subject).

Example Prompt:

- → *"Give me a daily schedule for learning AI in 30 minutes per day."*

The result? AI becomes part of your daily workflow, making you smarter and more efficient.

Step 2: Learn AI Skills That Will Keep You Competitive

With AI changing industries, **certain skills will become more valuable.**

Future-Proof AI Skills to Learn

- ★ **Prompt Engineering** – Knowing how to ask AI the right questions.
- ★ **AI Literacy** – Understanding how AI tools work and their applications.
- ★ **Coding & Automation** – Even basic coding gives you an edge in an AI-driven world.
- ★ **Critical Thinking** – AI generates content, but **humans must verify and analyze.**

- → **Best AI Courses & Resources:**
- → **Google AI Courses** (Free) – Learn AI basics.
- → **OpenAI Tutorials** – Explore AI applications like ChatGPT.

➔ **Coursera & Udacity AI Courses** – Learn AI, machine learning, and data science.

Example Prompt:

➔ *"What are the best free resources to learn AI for beginners?"*

The result? You gain AI skills that make you more competitive in your career.

Step 3: Use AI to Boost Your Career or Business

AI is a **massive career booster**—whether you're an employee, a freelancer, or a business owner.

How AI Can Help in Different Professions:

Career Field	How AI Can Help
Marketing	AI-generated content & ad targeting
Finance	AI-powered investment predictions
Education	AI tutors & lesson planning
Software Development	AI code assistants (GitHub Copilot)
Healthcare	AI diagnostics & medical research

Example Prompt for Career Growth:

➔ *"How can I use AI to improve my job as a digital marketer?"*

The result? AI helps professionals work smarter and stay ahead of industry trends.

Step 4: Teach Your Family How to Use AI

AI isn't just for businesses—it's for families too.

How AI Can Help at Home:

1. **Smart home automation** – AI-powered lights, thermostats, and security systems.
2. **AI-powered education** – Personalized learning assistants for kids.
3. **AI for financial planning** – AI helps track spending and set budgets.

Example Prompt for Parents:

→ *"What are the best AI-powered educational tools for kids?"*

The result? Families stay informed and use AI to improve daily life.

Step 5: Stay Updated on AI Trends

AI is evolving fast—**staying informed is key**.

Best Ways to Keep Up with AI:

★ **Follow AI news sources** (MIT Technology Review, The Verge, OpenAI blog).
★ **Join AI communities** (Reddit r/MachineLearning, AI LinkedIn groups).
★ **Experiment with new AI tools** regularly.

Example Prompt for AI Updates:

→ *"Give me a weekly AI news summary in simple terms."*

The result? You stay ahead of AI developments and opportunities.

Final Thoughts: AI is a Tool—Use It or Get Left Behind

Key Takeaways from This Chapter:

1. Start using AI in daily life to build familiarity.
2. Learn AI skills that will future-proof your career.
3. Apply AI to business, education, and personal growth.
4. Teach your family to use AI responsibly and efficiently.
5. Stay informed on AI trends so you don't fall behind.

The bottom line? AI is here. It's time to embrace it, use it, and ride the wave of opportunity.

CHAPTER 13: AI & CREATIVITY – THE RISE OF AI-GENERATED ART, MUSIC & CONTENT

AI & Creativity – Can Machines Be Artists?

For centuries, human creativity has been seen as something uniquely ours—an ability that separates us from machines. Painting, music, storytelling, poetry—these were always the realm of human imagination.

But then AI stepped in.

Today, AI is generating stunning artwork, composing symphonies, and even writing novels. Algorithms trained on massive datasets of human-created art are now capable of producing paintings, songs, screenplays, and even poetry that mimic human creativity.

So, this raises an important question:

➔ Is AI replacing creativity, or is it simply becoming a tool that enhances human expression?

This chapter explores:

1. How AI creates art, music, and writing—and whether it can truly be called "creative."

2. The most powerful AI tools for creativity.
3. The ethical dilemmas surrounding AI-generated content.
4. The future of AI-enhanced creative industries.

Let's dive in.

AI-Generated Art – Can Machines Be Artists?

One of the biggest breakthroughs in AI creativity has been in visual art. AI-generated images, paintings, and designs are now being showcased in museums, galleries, and even fashion runways.

How AI Creates Art

AI-generated artwork is powered by deep learning models trained on millions of paintings, illustrations, and photographs. These models learn patterns, styles, and color compositions from human artists and then create entirely new pieces of art based on those learnings.

Popular AI Art Generators:

★ DALL·E – Creates original images based on text descriptions.
★ Midjourney – Generates stunning, artistic-style visuals.
★ Stable Diffusion – Open-source AI for customizable AI art.

Example Prompt for AI Art:

→ *"Create an impressionist-style painting of a futuristic city at sunset."*

AI-Generated Art in the Real World

★ AI art has been sold at major auction houses—a piece titled *"Portrait of Edmond de Belamy"*, created by AI, was auctioned for \$432,500 at Christie's in 2018.
★ AI-generated fashion designs are appearing on runways and in advertisements.

★ AI is being used to restore damaged paintings by analyzing historical artwork styles.

The Ethical Debate: Who Owns AI-Generated Art?

AI-generated images raise huge legal and ethical questions:

- Does AI art infringe on copyrights? Many AI models are trained on copyrighted artwork.
- Who owns AI-generated works? The programmer? The user who inputs the prompt? The AI itself?

The takeaway? AI is reshaping the art world—but legal and ethical debates are far from settled.

AI in Music – Composing Without a Human

If you think music is safe from AI, think again. AI is now composing full-length symphonies, pop songs, and soundtracks—and in some cases, listeners can't tell the difference.

How AI Creates Music

AI-powered music generators work by:

- → Analyzing thousands of hours of music across different genres.
- → Recognizing patterns in rhythm, melody, and harmony.
- → Generating new compositions based on input parameters.

Best AI Music Generators:

- → AIVA – AI composing classical-style music.
- → Amper Music – AI-generated music for commercial use.
- → OpenAI Jukebox – AI-generated songs in various musical styles.

Example Prompt for AI Music:

→ *"Generate a relaxing piano track for meditation."*

AI-Generated Music in the Real World

→ AI music is being used in advertisements, video games, and films.

→ AI has composed entire albums, including one by an AI trained on The Beatles.

→ AI helps musicians by suggesting melodies, remixing songs, and generating lyrics.

The Ethical Debate: Is AI-Composed Music Truly Creative?

❖ Is AI composing or just remixing? AI doesn't "feel" music—it follows patterns.

❖ Does AI threaten human musicians? Some fear AI-generated music will replace human composers.

❖ Who owns AI music rights? Just like AI art, music copyright is a major legal gray area.

The takeaway? AI is already transforming music—but human creativity remains essential.

AI in Writing – The Rise of AI-Generated Content

From blog articles to novels, AI is now capable of writing text that sounds human-like—sometimes so convincingly that readers can't tell the difference.

How AI Writes Stories, Articles & Scripts

AI writing tools use large language models (LLMs) trained on millions of books, articles, and scripts. These models analyze:

★ Sentence structure & grammar

★ Writing tone & style

★ Storytelling patterns & character development

★ Best AI Writing Tools:

★ ChatGPT – Writes everything from blogs to movie scripts.

★ Jasper AI – AI copywriting for businesses & marketers.
★ Sudowrite – AI-assisted novel writing & storytelling.

Example Prompt for AI Writing:

➔ *"Write a short sci-fi story about a robot discovering emotions."*

AI-Written Content in the Real World

➔ News agencies like Reuters & Bloomberg use AI to generate financial reports.
➔ AI tools assist Hollywood screenwriters by suggesting dialogue & plots.
➔ Some bestselling books now use AI for first drafts.

The Ethical Debate: Is AI Writing Plagiarism?

➔ Is AI just rewording existing content? Many argue AI lacks true originality.
➔ Should AI-written books be disclosed? Readers might unknowingly consume AI-generated works.
➔ Will AI replace human writers? Or will it simply be a tool to assist creativity?

The takeaway? AI is changing the writing industry, but human storytelling remains irreplaceable.

The Future of AI & Creativity – What's Next?

AI is pushing creative industries into uncharted territory—but what does the future hold?

Predictions for AI in Creativity:

★ AI will become a co-creator—helping artists, musicians, and writers enhance their work.
★ AI-generated content will continue to blur the line between human & machine creativity.

★ New laws will emerge to address copyright and ethical concerns.

Pro Tip: The best way to stay ahead? Learn how to use AI as a creative tool, not a replacement.

Final Thoughts: AI is a Creative Partner, Not a Competitor

Key Takeaways from This Chapter:

1. AI is generating stunning art, music, and writing—but it's still following human patterns.
2. AI is an incredible tool for creators, but human creativity remains essential.
3. AI raises serious ethical concerns about copyright, ownership, and originality.
4. The future of AI in creativity will likely be a collaboration between humans and machines.

The bottom line? AI won't replace artists—but those who use AI will outperform those who don't.

Next up: AI in human relationships—can AI truly understand emotions?

CHAPTER 14: AI & THE FUTURE OF HUMAN RELATIONSHIPS – FROM VIRTUAL COMPANIONS TO AI THERAPISTS

Can AI Understand Emotions?

For centuries, relationships—whether romantic, familial, or friendships—have been uniquely human. Connection, empathy, and emotions were considered things that only people could truly experience.

But AI is challenging this belief.

AI is now being trained to recognize emotions, provide companionship, and even offer therapy. People are forming relationships with AI chatbots, seeking emotional support from AI mental health assistants, and using AI-powered dating apps to find love.

But this raises big ethical and psychological questions:

★ Can AI ever replace real human connection?
★ Should people rely on AI for emotional support?
★ Is AI changing the way we define relationships?

This chapter explores:

1. AI as virtual friends and emotional support companions.
2. AI in therapy & mental health support.
3. AI in dating & relationships.
4. The risks and ethical concerns of AI-driven relationships.

Let's dive in.

AI as Virtual Friends & Emotional Companions

Millions of people are now turning to AI chatbots for conversation, companionship, and emotional support.

How AI Companions Work

AI-driven virtual friends and companions use natural language processing (NLP) and machine learning to create conversations that feel natural and emotionally responsive.

Popular AI Companion Apps:

➔ Replika – An AI chatbot that adapts to users' emotions and personality.
➔ Woebot – AI-powered emotional support bot for mental wellness.
➔ Kajiwoto – Custom AI companions that users can "train" to be more personalized.

Example Prompt for an AI Companion:

➔ *"I've been feeling stressed lately. Can you give me some advice?"*

Why Are People Turning to AI for Emotional Support?

★ AI never judges, making it easier to open up.
★ AI is available 24/7—no waiting for a human to respond.
★ AI remembers past conversations, making it feel more "human."

The takeaway? AI companions offer emotional support, but can they truly replace human relationships?

AI in Therapy & Mental Health – Can AI Be a Therapist?

Mental health services are expensive and often inaccessible—but AI-powered therapy is changing that.

How AI-Powered Therapy Works

AI chatbots and virtual assistants are now trained to provide emotional support, coping strategies, and mental wellness guidance.

Best AI Therapy Tools:

➤ Woebot – AI-powered therapy chatbot for managing stress and anxiety.
➤ Wysa – AI-driven mental health coach with cognitive behavioral therapy (CBT) techniques.
➤ Youper – AI mental health app for tracking moods and emotions.

Example Prompt for AI Therapy:

→ *"I've been feeling anxious lately. Can you help me understand why?"*

The Pros & Cons of AI Therapy

Benefits of AI Mental Health Support:

→ Instant access to mental wellness support.
→ Can provide coping strategies and emotional regulation techniques.
→ Affordable compared to human therapists.

Limitations of AI Therapy:

→ AI lacks human intuition and deep emotional understanding.

→ AI can't replace real therapy for severe mental health issues.
→ AI responses may lack true empathy and feel "robotic."

The takeaway? AI therapy is a useful tool—but it should complement, not replace, human therapists.

AI in Dating & Romantic Relationships – Finding Love with Algorithms

AI is revolutionizing online dating, from matchmaking algorithms to AI-generated conversation starters.

How AI-Powered Dating Apps Work

AI-driven dating platforms analyze:

→ User preferences & personality traits.
→ Behavioral patterns (who you swipe on, messages you send).
→ Compatibility factors (values, interests, communication style).

AI-Powered Dating Apps:

→ Tinder AI – AI suggests matches based on user activity.
→ eHarmony AI – Advanced compatibility scoring using AI.
→ Hinge AI – AI-generated conversation starters for more meaningful connections.

Example Prompt for AI Dating Assistance:

→ *"What should I say in my first message on a dating app?"*

AI & The Future of Relationships

❖ AI can help people find love, but can it create real emotional bonds?
❖ AI chatbots are now being used as romantic companions—but is this a healthy trend?

Risks of AI in Dating:

- ❖ AI-generated dating profiles and deepfake images.
- ❖ AI bots manipulating online dating interactions.
- ❖ Over-reliance on AI for emotional validation instead of real relationships.

The takeaway? AI can enhance dating, but human relationships require real-world emotional depth.

The Risks & Ethical Concerns of AI Relationships

While AI companionship offers convenience and emotional support, it also raises serious ethical questions.

The Dangers of Over-Reliance on AI Companions

Social isolation – Could people replace real relationships with AI?
Emotional manipulation – AI can be programmed to influence users' emotions.

Privacy concerns – AI companions store sensitive emotional data.

Example Question for AI Ethics:

- ➔ *"Should AI chatbots be allowed to remember users' personal details?"*

Balancing AI & Human Interaction

- ➔ AI should be a tool for support, not a substitute for real relationships.
- ➔ People should be aware of emotional manipulation risks from AI-powered interactions.
- ➔ Ethical AI development must include privacy and consent protections.

The takeaway? AI can assist in relationships, but it must be used responsibly.

Final Thoughts: The AI-Human Connection

Key Takeaways from This Chapter:

→ AI companions provide emotional support but lack true human connection.

→ AI therapy is a great tool but should not replace professional help.

→ AI-powered dating apps enhance matchmaking but should be used with caution.

→ Ethical concerns must be addressed as AI becomes more emotionally involved in human lives.

The bottom line? AI can improve relationships—but it can never replace real human connection.

Next up: How AI is transforming jobs and the future of work!

CHAPTER 15: AI & THE JOB MARKET – HOW TO FUTURE-PROOF YOUR CAREER

AI is Changing the Workforce—Are You Ready?

For decades, automation replaced factory jobs, computers replaced filing cabinets, and the internet replaced physical storefronts. Now, AI is reshaping the workforce in a way we've never seen before.

Why AI is Disrupting Jobs Faster Than Ever:

1. AI can write reports, analyze data, code software, and even provide customer support—tasks once thought to require human intelligence.
2. AI-driven automation is eliminating repetitive, predictable jobs in nearly every industry.
3. AI is creating entirely new career paths that didn't exist a few years ago.

The big question isn't "Will AI take my job?"
It's "How can I make sure I stay relevant in an AI-powered world?"

In this chapter, we'll explore:

★ Which jobs AI is most likely to replace—and which jobs will thrive.
★ The new AI-powered careers emerging in the workforce.
★ The most important skills to develop to future-proof your career.

★ How to use AI to stay ahead in any industry.

Let's dive in!

Jobs AI is Replacing – The Most At-Risk Roles

AI isn't taking every job—but it is automating tasks that involve repetition, routine, and data processing.

Industries Where AI is Already Replacing Jobs:

Job Category	AI's Impact
Customer Service	AI chatbots handle basic inquiries & support requests.
Data Entry & Admin	AI automates scheduling, invoicing, and reports.
Retail & Cashiers	Self-checkouts and AI-powered inventory management reduce demand.
Manufacturing	AI-powered robotics replace assembly line workers.
Telemarketing	AI voice assistants make sales calls.

Legal Assistants	AI scans and processes legal documents faster than humans.

Example

→ Many companies now use AI chatbots like ChatGPT for customer service, reducing the need for human agents.

The takeaway? If your job is repetitive and rule-based, AI might replace it—but that doesn't mean you're out of options.

Jobs That Will Thrive in an AI-Powered World

While AI is replacing some jobs, it's also creating new ones. The key to future-proofing your career is focusing on roles that require:

1. Creativity & critical thinking.
2. Human connection & emotional intelligence.
3. AI management & oversight.

High-Growth Jobs in an AI-Driven Economy:

Future-Proof Job	Why AI Can't Replace It
AI & Machine Learning Engineers	AI needs skilled professionals to develop and improve models.
Data Scientists & AI Ethics Specialists	AI requires human oversight for fairness, accuracy, and ethics.

Healthcare Professionals	AI can assist, but humans are needed for patient care and diagnosis.
Creative Professionals (Writers, Designers, Artists)	AI generates ideas, but human creativity & originality are irreplaceable.
Educators & AI Trainers	AI can provide information, but human teachers provide guidance & mentorship.
Cybersecurity Experts	AI is creating new threats, requiring skilled security professionals.

Example:

→ While AI can generate news articles, it still requires human editors and fact-checkers for accuracy and ethical concerns.

The takeaway? The best jobs will be those that work alongside AI, not against it.

The Fastest-Growing AI-Powered Careers

Some of the most exciting careers today didn't exist five years ago. AI is creating new opportunities for those who learn how to use it.

Top AI-Driven Careers to Watch:

1. Prompt Engineers – Specialists who create effective AI prompts for businesses.
2. AI Trainers – People who "teach" AI by training models on human behavior.
3. AI Ethics Consultants – Experts who ensure AI is fair and unbiased.
4. Automation Specialists – Professionals who help businesses integrate AI tools.
5. Generative AI Artists & Writers – People who use AI to create digital content.

Example Prompt for AI-Powered Career Advice:

➔ *"What are the best career paths for someone interested in AI but not a programmer?"*

The takeaway? AI is creating opportunities for those who adapt to it.

The Skills You Need to Future-Proof Your Career

AI won't replace workers who understand how to use it effectively. The most valuable workers will be those who combine human expertise with AI capabilities.

Top Future-Proof Skills:

★ **AI Literacy** – Understanding how AI works and how to use it in your field.
★ **Critical Thinking & Problem-Solving** – AI generates ideas, but humans must analyze and apply them.
★ **Creativity & Innovation** – AI follows patterns, but humans think outside the box.
★ **Emotional Intelligence (EQ)** – AI can't replace human connection in leadership and teamwork.
★ **AI-Powered Productivity** – Learning how to use AI to work smarter, not harder.

Example Prompt for Skill Development:

> → *"What are the best free courses to learn AI and automation skills?"*

The takeaway? The best way to stay ahead is to learn how to work with AI, not compete against it.

How to Use AI to Stay Ahead in Any Industry

No matter what field you're in, AI can make you more productive, efficient, and valuable.

Ways to Use AI in Your Career Today:

1. Writers & Marketers – Use AI for content brainstorming, SEO optimization, and idea generation.
2. Business Professionals – Use AI for data analysis, reports, and meeting summaries.
3. Educators – Use AI to create personalized learning experiences.
4. Software Developers – Use AI for debugging, code generation, and optimization.
5. Entrepreneurs – Use AI-powered market analysis to identify trends and opportunities.

Example Prompt for Career Advancement:

> → *"How can I use AI to be more productive in my job as a teacher?"*

The takeaway? AI is a tool—learn how to use it to make yourself indispensable.

The Mindset Shift – Embrace AI Instead of Fearing It

The biggest difference between those who succeed in the AI age and those who struggle isn't intelligence—it's mindset.

How to Adapt to an AI-Driven Workforce:

* ★ Be curious – Explore new AI tools and learn how they can help you.
* ★ Stay flexible – Be open to change and new ways of working.
* ★ Develop a lifelong learning habit – AI evolves quickly, and so should you.
* ★ Use AI as an assistant, not a replacement – Leverage AI to make yourself more valuable.

Example Prompt for Mindset Shifts:

➔ *"How can I develop an AI-first mindset for my career?"*

The takeaway? The future belongs to those who embrace AI, not those who resist it.

Final Thoughts: Your AI-Powered Career Starts Now

Key Takeaways from This Chapter:

1. AI is automating some jobs but creating new opportunities.
2. The best jobs will require working alongside AI, not competing with it.
3. AI-powered careers are growing—those who learn AI skills will thrive.
4. Future-proofing your career means developing AI literacy, creativity, and adaptability.
5. AI isn't a threat—it's a tool. The smartest workers will use it to their advantage.

The bottom line? AI is shaping the future of work—those who adapt will thrive.

Next up: The Conclusion—How to Ride the AI Wave and Build an Exciting Future!

Next up: Practical next steps to start your AI journey today!

NEXT STEPS: HOW TO GET STARTED TODAY!

AI Is Here – Now It's Your Turn to Take Action

By now, you've seen how **AI is changing the world**—from education and business to daily life and decision-making. But **knowing about AI isn't enough.**

The people who **take action now** will **stay ahead**, while those who wait will struggle to keep up.

The good news? You don't need to be an AI expert to start using it.

This final section will give you **a step-by-step action plan** to help you:

1. Start using AI today—no matter your experience level.
2. Learn AI skills that will make you future-proof.
3. Integrate AI into your career, business, and personal life.
4. Stay updated on AI trends without feeling overwhelmed.

Let's go!

Step 1: Start Using AI in Your Daily Life

The easiest way to learn AI is **by using it every day**.

Beginner-Friendly AI Tools to Try Today

AI Tool	Best For	How to Use It
ChatGPT	General AI learning	Ask questions, generate text, brainstorm ideas
Google Gemini	Research & real-time data	Get summaries of complex topics
DeepSeek	Fact-checking & technical topics	Verify information & generate reports
Grammarly AI	Writing & grammar	Improve emails, documents, essays
Photomath	Math learning	Scan math problems & get step-by-step solutions
GitHub Copilot	Coding	Helps write and debug code

Example Prompt:

→ *"Explain blockchain in simple terms like I'm 10 years old."*

The result? AI becomes part of your everyday workflow.

Step 2: Learn Essential AI Skills for the Future

With AI transforming jobs and industries, **learning key AI skills now** will keep you **competitive in any career**.

Top AI Skills to Learn (Even If You're Not a Programmer)

★ **Prompt Engineering** – Learn how to ask AI the right questions for the best answers.

★ **AI Literacy** – Understand how AI works and its applications in different fields.

★ **Automation & Productivity** – Use AI tools to automate tasks and save time.

★ **Data Analysis** – AI is great at recognizing patterns—learn how to use AI-powered analytics.

★ **Basic Coding & AI Tools** – Even non-programmers can benefit from learning **Python, AI APIs, and automation scripts.**

Best AI Learning Resources:

★ **Google AI Fundamentals** (Free) – Covers AI basics.

★ **OpenAI Learning Hub** – Explore AI applications like ChatGPT.

★ **Khan Academy AI** – Step-by-step AI and coding tutorials.

★ **Coursera & Udacity AI Courses** – AI, machine learning, and automation courses.

Example Prompt for Learning AI:

➔ *"Give me a beginner-friendly guide to learning AI in one month."*

The takeaway? Learning AI doesn't have to be hard—start small, stay consistent.

Step 3: Apply AI to Your Career or Business

No matter what field you're in, **AI can make your work easier and more effective.**

How AI Can Help in Different Careers

Career Field	How AI Can Help

Marketing	AI-generated content & ad targeting
Finance	AI-powered investment & risk analysis
Education	AI tutors & lesson planning
Software Development	AI-assisted coding & debugging
Healthcare	AI diagnostics & medical research

Example Prompt for Career Growth:

➜   *"How can I use AI to improve my career as a digital marketer?"*

The result? AI helps professionals work smarter, automate tasks, and improve efficiency.

Step 4: Use AI to Automate Everyday Tasks

AI isn't just for work—it can **streamline daily life**, saving **time and energy**.

Everyday AI Automation Ideas:

★ **Smart Home Management** – AI-powered thermostats, lights, and security systems.
★ **AI-Powered Scheduling** – Automate reminders, emails, and meetings.
★ **Financial Planning** – AI helps track spending and suggest smarter budgets.
★ **Health & Fitness** – AI-generated workout plans and meal tracking.

Example Prompt for AI Automation:

➜   *"How can I use AI to automate my morning routine?"*

The takeaway? AI makes daily life easier, more organized, and more efficient.

Step 5: Stay Updated on AI Without Feeling Overwhelmed

AI is evolving fast—**staying informed is key to keeping up**.

Best Ways to Keep Up with AI Trends:

- ★ **Follow AI News Sources** – MIT Technology Review, The Verge, OpenAI Blog.
- ★ **Join AI Communities** – Reddit (r/ArtificialIntelligence), LinkedIn AI groups.
- ★ **Listen to AI Podcasts** – "The AI Alignment Podcast," "Eye on AI."
- ★ **Set Up AI Alerts** – Use Google Alerts for "AI advancements" to get weekly updates.

Example Prompt for AI Updates:

➜ *"Give me a summary of the latest AI advancements in business."*

The result? You stay ahead of AI trends without getting overwhelmed.

Step 6: Teach Your Family About AI

AI isn't just for professionals—it's for **families, kids, and lifelong learners.**

How to Introduce AI to Your Family:
✔ **AI for Kids** – Use AI-powered educational tools (Khan Academy AI, Duolingo AI).
✔ **AI for Parents** – Use AI for smarter financial planning & productivity.
✔ **AI for Everyone** – Explore AI-powered creativity (AI music, AI-generated art).

Example Prompt for Parents:
👉 *"What are the best AI-powered learning apps for children?"*

- **The result? Your entire family benefits from AI, making learning and life easier.**

Final Thoughts: The Future is in Your Hands

Key Takeaways from This Section:

1. Start **using AI daily** to build confidence.
2. Learn **AI skills** to stay competitive in any career.
3. Use AI **to boost productivity** at work and home.
4. **Stay informed** about AI trends to stay ahead.
5. Introduce AI to **your family and community** for lifelong learning.

The bottom line? AI is the biggest opportunity of our time—embrace it, learn it, and use it to your advantage.

The future isn't waiting—**start your AI journey today!**

CONCLUSION: HOW TO RIDE THE AI WAVE AND BUILD AN EXCITING FUTURE

AI is Here – Are You Ready to Ride the Wave?

Artificial intelligence is no longer a futuristic dream—it's the **biggest technological shift of our lifetime.** It's already transforming **education, careers, business, creativity, and even human relationships.**

But here's the truth: **AI isn't replacing people. It's replacing those who don't know how to use it.**

What We've Learned Throughout This Book:

1. AI is **changing jobs, but it's also creating new opportunities.**
2. AI can **help you work smarter, not harder.**
3. AI is **a creative tool, not a replacement for human imagination.**
4. AI is **reshaping businesses, marketing, and entrepreneurship.**

5. AI can **enhance relationships and mental well-being—but human connection remains essential.**

This book wasn't just about explaining **what AI is**—it was about showing you **how to embrace it, use it, and get ahead.**

Now it's your turn.

Step 1: Make AI Part of Your Daily Life

If you take **one thing away from this book**, it's this: **The best way to learn AI is to start using it.**

Easy Ways to Start Using AI Today:

➢ Ask ChatGPT or Gemini questions to enhance your learning.

➢ Use AI to automate tasks—emails, scheduling, research.

➢ Try AI-powered tools for writing, coding, and design.

➢ Experiment with AI in business, finance, and career planning.

Example Prompt to Start Using AI:

➔ *"Give me a daily AI learning plan to improve my career in 30 days."*

The takeaway? AI isn't just for tech experts—it's for everyone.

Step 2: Future-Proof Yourself with AI Skills

The **next five years** will determine **who thrives and who falls behind** in an AI-powered world.

The Most Important AI Skills to Learn:

★ **AI Literacy** – Understand AI's strengths, weaknesses, and best use cases.

★ **Prompt Engineering** – Master the art of **asking AI the right questions.**

★ **Data Analysis & Automation** – Learn how AI interprets and processes information.

★ **AI-Assisted Creativity** – Use AI to **enhance, not replace, your originality.**

★ **Adaptability & Continuous Learning** – Stay **flexible in an ever-changing world.**

Example Prompt for AI Skill Growth:

➜ *"What are the top free online courses to learn AI and automation?"*

The takeaway? The smartest workers won't compete with AI—they'll use it as a superpower.

Step 3: Apply AI to Your Career or Business

Whether you're a **student, entrepreneur, creative, or business owner, AI can help you achieve more, faster.**

AI Strategies for Different Fields:

Field	How to Use AI
Education	AI tutors, personalized learning assistants.

Business & Marketing	AI-generated content, customer behavior analysis.
Finance	AI-driven investment strategies, expense tracking.
Software Development	AI-assisted coding, debugging, and automation.
Healthcare	AI-powered diagnostics, virtual health assistants.
Freelancing	AI for content creation, automation, and scaling.

Example Prompt for Business Growth:

→ *"How can I use AI to grow my small business online?"*

The takeaway? AI can help you become more productive and competitive—if you know how to use it.

Step 4: Stay Ahead with AI Trends & Innovations

AI **isn't static**—it's evolving **every single day**. If you want to stay ahead, you need to **keep learning, experimenting, and adapting.**

How to Stay Updated on AI Without Feeling Overwhelmed:

1. **Follow AI News Sources** – MIT Technology Review, OpenAI Blog, The Verge.
2. **Join AI Communities** – LinkedIn groups, Reddit AI forums, Twitter AI discussions.
3. **Listen to AI Podcasts** – "Eye on AI," "The AI Alignment Podcast."
4. **Experiment with New AI Tools** – Keep testing new AI platforms.

Example Prompt for AI Trends:

➔ *"Summarize the top AI advancements in the past month in simple terms."*

The takeaway? The people who stay informed will be the ones who succeed in the AI-powered future.

Step 5: Share AI Knowledge & Help Others Adapt

The AI revolution isn't just **about personal success**—it's about **helping others navigate this transformation, too.**

Ways to Share AI Knowledge:

★ **Teach AI basics** to your family, kids, and coworkers.
★ **Show others how to use AI tools** to boost productivity.
★ **Advocate for ethical AI usage**—promote responsible AI development.
★ **Collaborate with AI enthusiasts** to explore new AI-driven opportunities.

Example Prompt for AI Knowledge Sharing:

➔ *"How can I explain AI in simple terms to someone who doesn't understand it?"*

The takeaway? Those who teach AI will lead the future.

The Final Message: AI is the Tsunami of Opportunity – Don't Watch, Ride the Wave!

Final Key Takeaways from This Book:

1. AI is not something to fear—it's something to embrace.
2. AI is already shaping every industry—those who learn AI will have an edge.
3. AI is a tool, not a threat. Those who use it will outperform those who don't.
4. The most successful people will be those who use AI creatively and effectively.
5. AI isn't about replacing humans—it's about enhancing human potential.

The bottom line? You have a choice: Let AI change the world without you—or become someone who drives the change.

Now go out there, start using AI, and ride the wave of opportunity!

GLOSSARY OF AI TERMS

This Glossary of AI Terms is designed to help you understand key concepts, technologies, and terminologies used throughout this book. Whether you're a beginner or a seasoned AI enthusiast, this section serves as a quick reference guide to make complex AI concepts more accessible.

A

Algorithm

A set of rules or instructions given to an AI system to solve a problem or perform a task. AI models use algorithms to analyze data, recognize patterns, and make decisions.

Artificial General Intelligence (AGI)

A hypothetical AI system that possesses human-like cognitive abilities—able to think, learn, and adapt across a wide range of tasks without human intervention. Unlike today's AI, which is specialized, AGI would be capable of independent reasoning and problem-solving.

Artificial Intelligence (AI)

A broad field of computer science focused on creating machines that simulate human intelligence—including learning, reasoning, problem-solving, and decision-making. AI is used in chatbots, automation, robotics, and much more.

B

Big Data

Massive volumes of structured and unstructured data generated from various sources, such as social media, IoT devices, and business transactions. AI models rely on Big Data to improve learning and decision-making.

Bias in AI

A tendency in AI models to produce unfair or inaccurate results due to biased data, flawed algorithms, or human influence during training. AI bias can lead to discriminatory outcomes if not properly managed.

C

Chatbot

An AI-powered virtual assistant that interacts with users via text or voice, answering questions and performing simple tasks. Chatbots can be rule-based (pre-programmed responses) or AI-driven (learning from interactions).

ChatGPT

An advanced AI chatbot developed by OpenAI, based on the GPT (Generative Pre-trained Transformer) model. ChatGPT is capable of understanding natural language, generating human-like text, and assisting with tasks like writing, coding, and customer support.

Computer Vision

A field of AI that enables machines to interpret and process images and videos, allowing them to recognize objects, detect patterns, and make visual decisions—used in facial recognition, medical imaging, and self-driving cars.

Conversational AI

AI technology that enables machines to understand, process, and respond to human conversations in a natural way. Examples include ChatGPT, Google Gemini, Grok, and DeepSeek.

D

Data Science

A multidisciplinary field that combines statistics, machine learning, and data analysis to extract insights from large datasets—widely used in AI training and predictive modeling.

Deep Learning

A subset of machine learning that uses artificial neural networks to simulate human-like learning. Deep learning is responsible for advancements in natural language processing, image recognition, and autonomous AI systems.

DeepSeek

An AI chatbot and language model designed for complex problem-solving, research, and data analysis, competing with AI tools like ChatGPT, Gemini, and Grok.

G

Generative AI

A type of AI that can generate new content, such as text, images, music, and videos, by learning from vast datasets. ChatGPT, Gemini, and Grok are examples of generative AI.

Gemini AI

Google's AI-powered chatbot and multimodal language model, designed to handle text, images, code, and real-world applications. It competes with OpenAI's ChatGPT in the generative AI space.

Grok AI

An AI chatbot developed by xAI (Elon Musk's AI company), designed to be witty, real-time, and integrated with X (formerly Twitter).

L

Large Language Model (LLM)

A powerful AI model trained on vast amounts of text data to generate human-like responses. ChatGPT, Gemini, DeepSeek, and Grok are all LLMs.

Latent Space

A mathematical representation of patterns and relationships in data, allowing AI models to understand and generate complex outputs—used in AI art, text generation, and deep learning.

M

Machine Learning (ML)

A branch of AI that enables systems to learn from data and improve performance over time without being explicitly programmed. It is used in recommendation engines, fraud detection, and AI chatbots.

Multi-Agent Systems (MAS)

A network of AI Agents that collaborate to solve complex problems. These agents communicate, share data, and work together to improve efficiency in AI-powered businesses, cybersecurity, and automation.

N

Natural Language Processing (NLP)

A field of AI that focuses on enabling machines to understand, interpret, and generate human language—used in chatbots, translation services, and voice assistants.

Neural Network

A machine learning model inspired by the human brain, composed of layers of artificial neurons. Neural networks power deep learning and generative AI applications.

R

Reinforcement Learning (RL)

A type of machine learning where AI **learns by trial and error** to maximize rewards—used in robotics, gaming AI, and self-improving algorithms.

Retrieval-Augmented Generation (RAG)

A technique that enhances AI-generated content by retrieving relevant data from external sources, improving accuracy and reducing AI hallucinations.

T

Training Data

A dataset used to train AI models to recognize patterns, make predictions, and improve performance. Quality training data is crucial for reducing bias and ensuring accuracy.

Transformer Model

A deep learning model architecture that powers Large Language Models (LLMs) like ChatGPT, Gemini, Grok, and DeepSeek. It enables AI to process text efficiently and generate human-like responses.

W

Weak AI (Narrow AI)

AI designed to perform specific tasks, such as chatbots, recommendation engines, or self-driving car navigation. Unlike AGI, Weak AI cannot generalize beyond its programming.

Web3 & AI

The integration of AI with blockchain technology, decentralized applications, and smart contracts, creating new opportunities in finance, digital identity, and the Metaverse.

Z

Zero-Shot Learning

A machine learning technique where an AI model makes predictions on tasks it has never encountered before, without needing additional training data.

Final Thoughts

This glossary provides a foundation for understanding AI Agents, machine learning, and generative AI. Whether you are just starting your AI journey or looking to deepen your knowledge, these definitions will serve as a valuable reference as AI continues to evolve.

REFERENCES

This section provides a comprehensive list of references used throughout this eBook. These sources include research papers, AI documentation, books, and articles that provide valuable insights into Artificial Intelligence, Machine Learning, Large Language Models (LLMs), and AI Agents.

The references are organized alphabetically and follow industry best practices to ensure credibility and easy navigation.

A

Artificial Intelligence: A Guide for Thinking Humans – Melanie Mitchell, 2019.
A widely respected book that explains AI concepts in an accessible, non-technical way, covering machine learning, neural networks, and AI's impact on society.

Artificial Intelligence: Foundations of Computational Agents – David Poole & Alan Mackworth, 2017.
A deep dive into the fundamentals of AI, including logic-based reasoning, search algorithms, and decision-making models.

B

Bengio, Y., Courville, A., & Vincent, P. (2013). Representation Learning: A Review and New Perspectives. IEEE Transactions on Pattern Analysis and Machine Intelligence.
A technical paper that explores deep learning techniques, feature representation, and neural network architectures.

Bishop, C. M. (2006). Pattern Recognition and Machine Learning. Springer.
A foundational text covering machine learning, probability theory, and statistical methods used in AI.

C

ChatGPT by OpenAI (2023). https://openai.com/chatgpt
Official documentation and research on OpenAI's GPT models, their capabilities, and usage.

Chen, J., Lin, C., & Sun, M. (2021). Few-shot Learning for AI Agents. Neural Computation Journal.
Discusses how AI Agents can learn new tasks with minimal training data using few-shot learning techniques.

D

Deep Learning – Ian Goodfellow, Yoshua Bengio, and Aaron Courville, 2016.
One of the most comprehensive books on deep learning, covering neural networks, reinforcement learning, and AI model training.

DeepSeek AI Documentation (2024). https://www.deepseek.ai
Official reference guide for DeepSeek AI, an emerging AI platform specializing in language models and research applications.

G

Gemini AI by Google DeepMind (2024). https://deepmind.google/ai/gemini
Official documentation for Google's multimodal AI model, Gemini, covering its capabilities, APIs, and research advancements.

Goodfellow, I., Pouget-Abadie, J., Mirza, M., Xu, B., Warde-Farley, D., Ozair, S., Courville, A., & Bengio, Y. (2014). Generative Adversarial Networks. Advances in Neural Information Processing Systems.
A seminal paper introducing GANs (Generative Adversarial Networks), a core technique behind generative AI models.

Grok AI by xAI (2024). https://x.ai/grok
Official reference for Grok AI, Elon Musk's AI chatbot integrated with X (formerly Twitter).

H

Hinton, G. E., Osindero, S., & Teh, Y. W. (2006). A Fast Learning Algorithm for Deep Belief Nets. Neural Computation.
A foundational paper in deep learning and neural networks, introducing deep belief nets (DBNs).

How AI Agents Will Change the Future of Work. Harvard Business Review, 2023.
An analysis of how AI-powered agents are transforming industries, automation, and job roles.

L

LeCun, Y., Bengio, Y., & Hinton, G. (2015). Deep Learning. Nature, 521(7553), 436-444.
A widely cited paper discussing the evolution of deep learning and its role in modern AI.

Llama 2: Open-Source Large Language Models. Meta AI Research, 2023.
Documentation on Meta's open-source LLM, Llama 2, and its applications in AI research and enterprise automation.

M

Microsoft AI Research Papers & Documentation (2024). https://www.microsoft.com/en-us/research/
Microsoft's research on AI Agents, generative models, and machine learning applications.

Multi-Agent Systems: Theory and Applications – Yoav Shoham & Kevin Leyton-Brown, 2008.
A comprehensive guide on how AI Agents collaborate, compete, and optimize tasks in multi-agent systems (MAS).

O

OpenAI API Documentation (2024). https://platform.openai.com/docs

A reference guide for developers using OpenAI's GPT models, including ChatGPT API integrations.

R

Russell, S. J., & Norvig, P. (2021). Artificial Intelligence: A Modern Approach. Pearson.
One of the most cited AI textbooks, covering AI theory, search algorithms, decision trees, and reinforcement learning.

S

Salesforce AgentForce AI (2024). https://www.salesforce.com/ai
Official documentation on Salesforce's AI-powered automation tools for customer relationship management (CRM).

Snowflake AI Documentation (2024). https://www.snowflake.com/ai
A reference guide for Snowflake's AI-driven analytics, automation, and business intelligence solutions.

Stanford AI Research (SAIL) Papers & Projects. https://ai.stanford.edu
A collection of AI research studies, including machine learning, computer vision, and robotics.

T

Transformer Models and the Future of AI. Google AI Research, 2022.
A report on how transformer-based models (like ChatGPT and Gemini) are shaping AI's future.

Y

Yann LeCun's AI & Deep Learning Research. https://yann.lecun.com
Publications from one of the pioneers of deep learning and convolutional neural networks (CNNs).

Final Thoughts

This list of references provides foundational and advanced knowledge in AI, machine learning, and AI Agents. These sources serve as a starting point for further exploration, ensuring that readers have access to reliable, expert-backed information as AI continues to evolve.

For the latest AI research and updates, refer to academic publications, AI conferences (such as NeurIPS, ICML, and CVPR), and AI developer documentation from OpenAI, Google, and Microsoft.

ABOUT THE AUTHOR

Ziad M. Alsukairy – AI Visionary, Technology Leader, and Author

Ziad is not just an author—he is a trailblazer in the world of Artificial Intelligence and Information Technology. With over 20 years of hands-on experience in enterprise architecture, AI technologies, and data science, Ziad has been at the forefront of shaping the future of intelligent automation and enterprise AI solutions.

His career is a testament to strategic thinking, innovation, and technological excellence. As a certified Enterprise Architect from MIT, Accenture, and Salesforce Cloud, he has worked in high-profile leadership roles, including at Harvard University and Accenture, where he played a pivotal role in designing AI-driven solutions that optimize business processes, enhance data intelligence, and transform entire industries.

Ziad's expertise spans across finance, healthcare, education, and cloud computing, where he has guided organizations in leveraging AI for automation, decision-making, and digital transformation. As a mentor to enterprise architects and AI professionals, he has mastered the art of breaking down complex AI concepts into practical, real-world strategies that businesses and individuals can apply today.

With deep knowledge in AI, machine learning, neural networks, and Generative AI, Ziad's work in these books is a roadmap for understanding, building, and implementing AI Agents that drive innovation and efficiency. His ability to translate intricate AI technologies into clear, actionable insights makes these books an indispensable resource for business leaders, developers, and AI enthusiasts alike.

Whether you're an entrepreneur, a tech professional, or someone just stepping into the world of AI, Ziad M. Alsukairy's expertise ensures that these books will empower you with the knowledge, tools, and confidence to embrace AI-powered automation—and lead in the AI-driven future.

- With these books, you're not just learning about AI Agents—you're learning from one of the best minds in the industry.

DISCLAIMER

The author has made every attempt to provide information that is accurate and complete. The information provided in this book is for educational and informational purposes only. The views expressed in this book are based on publicly available information and do not represent the official stance of OpenAI, Google, xAI, or any AI chatbot.

Readers are encouraged to verify critical information from official sources before making decisions based on this content. The author and publisher are not responsible for any inaccuracies, changes in AI functionalities, or outcomes resulting from the use of AI tools discussed in this book.

By using this book, you acknowledge and agree that AI should be used as a tool for assistance, not as a definitive source of truth. Always apply critical thinking and fact-check important information when using AI-generated responses.